GHOSTS ALONG THE
NAVESINK AND
SHREWSBURY
RIVERS

GHOSTS ALONG THE
NAVESINK AND
SHREWSBURY
RIVERS

PATRICIA HEYER

Haunted
America

Published by Haunted America
A Division of The History Press
Charleston, SC
www.historypress.com

First published 2020

Manufactured in the United States

ISBN 9781467146425

Library of Congress Control Number: 2020938471

CONTENTS

INTRODUCTION

This is a book about ghosts—but not just any ghosts. It is an account of the folktales, unexplained events and ghostly encounters from the shores of our sister rivers, the Navesink and the Shrewsbury. These are the ghostly spirits with which we share this unique little area of Monmouth County known to many as the "land of the two rivers." These accounts have been harvested from a variety of historical archives, out of print publications, oral histories and shared folklore. The detailed historical background for each tale not only enriches the story line but also provides a clear frame of reference for the historical event and its consequences.

The Lenni Lenape referred to this land as Narvarumsunk, but for most of us, it is simply home. The five-mile-long and three-mile-wide peninsula includes the towns of Red Bank, Fair Haven, Rumson, Little Silver, Monmouth Beach and parts of Middletown and Shrewsbury. As the barrier beach serves as a border to the east, connected by several bridges, the area also includes Sea Bright and the remaining barrier beach from Monmouth Beach to Sandy Hook.

The local historical records of the two rivers and the peninsula offer evidence of the numerous and noteworthy contributions of this area to the history of our nation. It was here in our very backyard that democracy was born when locals found the American Revolution to be more of a civil war than a battle against England. It was here, during the Civil War, that Navarumsunk emerged as a grocery store for the Union army. Here, the budding steamboat era blossomed, the newly developing railroads expanded and the Industrial Revolution evolved into the age of technology. Beginning in 1920, the estuaries, coves, creeks and secluded docks were the centers of national civil disobedience against Prohibition, as rumrunning became a local industry. Even through two world wars, this region served as the front line against the enemy. Throughout its history, America has relied on these two rivers, the peninsula and the good people who call this place home. These two marine estuaries and their peninsula have contributed to and celebrated America's successes, as well as suffered the heartbreak of its tragedies.

At the same time, the number of written and oral reports of local paranormal activities has remained consistently elevated over the years. Much has been written about why there is so much paranormal and inexplicable activity in the area. Some authors claim it is the intense history of the region that stimulates the innumerable supernatural claims. Others insist that this connection with history coupled with the area's close affiliation with the ocean results in incalculable amounts of spontaneous energy in the area. They contend that the tremendous energy that comes from the Atlantic being the "graveyard of the sea" somehow fuses the area's historic energy, resulting in what some call a numen, or a place that has a spiritual or mystical energy of its own. Whatever the cause, we know there are countless records of apparitions, ghostly encounters, unexplained events and peculiar sightings across our region.

It is from these unique circumstances that these accounts have been gleaned. They are chronicles unique to this location and to our neighbors who have shared them with us. Within these pages, you will be introduced to the numerous forms of ghostly specters that you are likely to encounter here. You will meet spirits who refuse to leave, ghosts with unfinished business, specters who just want to say goodbye and some who just do not realize they are dead. There are accounts of apparitions floating on the Shrewsbury River, as well as those frozen in the ice of the Navesink River. There are unique and singular paranormal accounts from the Prohibition era, and there are peculiar accounts of a successful, yet seemingly haunted farm that once thrived along the Shrewsbury. You will visit cemeteries where the dead are not always at rest, and you will read tales of gruesome specters who invaded the Old Middletown Village. There is an account of a modern restaurant with a resident ghost, tales of a river monster observed by noted scientists, stories of a ghost with a police record and accounts of ghostly specters emanating from a local "oyster war."

These curious encounters that have been found along the Shrewsbury and Navesink are thought-provoking and make for absorbing reading. They not only highlight our colorful history, but they also link us with the unrestrained energy of the human spirit, exposing the intersection of history and the paranormal all around us. So, kick off your shoes, get comfortable and read on to learn more of the ghostly tales of our twin rivers.

1
GHOSTS OF THE
TWO RIVERS PENINSULA

The Two Rivers Peninsula, known to the Lenape Native Americans as Navarumsunk, is a five-mile-long and three-mile-wide stretch of land that separates the Navesink River in the north from the Shrewsbury in the south. Located to the east, alongside the two merging estuaries, is a narrow barrier beach, which stretches from Sea Bright to Sandy Hook. It is undoubtedly one of the most historic and beautiful spots in all of New Jersey, made even more special because it is our home.

Much has been written about our little neck of the woods in both history books and travel brochures. Just as we have welcomed countless visitors to our rivers and shores, we have also experienced a history that is unparalleled in intensity and richness. Who else can claim that the great battle for freedom and liberty was fought in their own backyard or that their hometown served as the grocery store for troops during the Civil War? We can't forget that it was our shores that were home to the civil disobedience of Prohibition and that served as the strategic line of defense during two world wars.

This peninsula indeed has an extremely rich and colorful history, so it is not surprising to know that it also has a prolific chronicle of paranormal activities, which include a host of ghostly sightings. It is not a new phenomenon; local people have shared personal paranormal accounts by word of mouth for nearly four centuries, and people are now sharing their personal accounts of peculiar happenings along the twin rivers. But what kind of supernatural events are we talking about? We are talking about the most commonly known and discussed of all paranormal experiences: ghosts. We're exploring those spirits that haunt the rolling green banks of the Navesink, the scenic marshy slopes of the Shrewsbury and the peninsula in between.

So, what exactly is a ghost? The answer to that depends largely on who you ask. Dictionary.com says that a ghost is "the soul of a dead person, a disembodied spirit, usually as a vague, shadowy or evanescent form, as wandering among or haunting living persons." But if you ask one hundred different people the same question, you will likely get one hundred different answers. At the same time, we all have a general agreement that ghosts are spirits of the deceased. We refer to them with a variety of names, such as ghosts, spirits, apparitions, specters, phantoms, spooks, wraiths, banshees, shadows and phantasms. We will likely not be able to agree on who or what ghosts are, where they came from, where they are going or, most of all, why we see them. The theories, explanations and hypotheses are as varied as the experts.

Spiritualists say that the human spirit survives after death and that ghosts are the souls of deceased individuals who, for some reason, have not passed on to the next plane of existence. Those with a great affinity for physics claim that it was Einstein who explained how ghosts can exist. This theory insists that, to understand ghosts, we must understand that the universe and everything in it is made of energy. Einstein stated, "Energy cannot be created or destroyed; it can only be changed from one form to another." So, when a human dies, their energy cannot just dissipate; it must go somewhere. By definition, then, energy that has departed the human body must move into another dimension of time or space.

There are countless explanations and theories about the origins or even definitions of a ghost. We can leave that debate to the philosophers, scientists and theologians. What we do know for certain is that a belief in ghosts and spirits has been part of the human condition since the beginning of recorded history. They have been identified on every continent of the globe and in every world culture, both ancient and modern. They are part of nearly every religion, philosophy and collection of folklore. We only need to glance at our society's fascination with the supernatural, as evidenced by the number of movies, television shows, magazines and books that are committed to it, to know that twenty-first-century humans are entranced by tales of ghostly specters.

What sort of specters are we likely to meet along the riverbanks and shores of the Navesink and Shrewsbury Rivers? One thing most students of the supernatural agree on is that not all ghosts are alike. It is a given that all ghosts are deceased, but just as with the living, individual ghosts have specific characteristics that make each one unique. Certain kinds of ghosts only make one appearance, while others are with us constantly. Some make no effort to communicate, while a few can't stop making noises. Several are obviously aware of their situation as ghosts, yet a number think they are still living. The cluster of ghostly specters we find along our riverbanks and shores fall into six broad categories. In this chapter, we will explore these groupings to identify their unique characteristics, and then we'll meet some of these specters with whom we share this peninsula.

MEET THE INTELLIGENT AND INTERACTIVE GHOSTS

As you travel throughout the two rivers region, intelligent and interactive ghosts are the kind you are most likely to encounter. These spirits demonstrate intelligence and have the ability to interact with humans. They may manifest as historical figures, loved ones or even intimate friends who have passed on. Frequently, they exhibit the same personality they had in life and demonstrate a wide range of emotions. These specters are anxious to make their presence known to humans. They do this by speaking, singing, making noises and, sometimes, by being visible. Often, you know this ghost is nearby due to its lingering scent; the specter's favorite cologne, cigar and even the aroma of specific foods can identify the spirit and let you know it is nearby.

The intelligent and interactive ghost interacts freely with the living. *From www.freerangestock.com.*

The guardian angel is a specific kind of intelligent ghost. This spirit exhibits a strong positive energy. It is known to linger near loved ones or appear to offer aid to those in distress. They watch out for and offer comfort to those they encounter. Some make their presence known, others remain invisible. Although most people assume this is a deceased ancestor or close friend, guardian angels have been known to be former caregivers and first responders, including policemen, firemen, teachers and nurses. These intelligent spirits have been recorded in significant numbers in the watershed region of the two rivers.

THREE BOYS AND A HOUSE POSSESSED

A Red Bank Haunting

Just a few doors down Front Street, near the Washington Street Historic District in Red Bank, there once stood a creepy old haunted house. Well, that is what the fifth graders at the nearby Mechanic Street School would have called it. The two-story white clapboard house had a wide wraparound porch, tall and narrow windows, dark shutters and a pair of paneled front doors. There was nothing spectacular about the house except for its delightful view of the Navesink River. The house was nestled between a similar home on its left and a funeral home on its right, and along its backyard fence sat the Mechanic Street School. The house is gone now; it was torn down in the late 1960s to make way for a yellow brick medical building.

The last resident of the house was an old woman who lived there alone for many years. The area's children only knew that she was old, stingy with candy on Halloween and, therefore, likely a witch. By the early 1960s, the house had fallen into disrepair. The sidewalk was cracked and the yard overgrown with quackgrass and weeds. The faded black shutters hung at odd angles off the side of the front windows. The paint had long since chipped and faded, leaving the house with a weather-worn and shoddy appearance.

The house stood vacant for quite some time. Before long, the abandoned building became a nuisance in the neighborhood and an attraction to vagrants and local kids. The old woman's property had never been claimed, so it remained there, along with what appeared to be her hoarder's collection of paper bags, magazines, old stuffed animals and dolls. It wasn't long before a rumor spread that the old lady had indeed been a witch and had left a curse on the house. If anyone entered the upstairs bedroom, where she died, it was said they would never be able to utter a word of what they had seen.

The principal at the local school, Miss McCue, admonished the students regularly about trespassing on the property. Any student seen on or near the property was immediately sent up to Miss McCue for a serious talking to. But fifth grade boys being fifth grade boys found this challenge irresistible. It began as a game of dare and double dare. At first, they would dare one another to just climb the porch steps. Once they had achieved that feat, the dares progressed to knocking on the door. From there, it advanced to pushing open the door and, finally, to stepping inside the house and walking down the long, dark hallway.

The house itself was laid out like many from its time period. Visitors stepped from the front door into a wide entrance hall. Along one side, there was a narrow wooden staircase that led to the second-floor bedrooms. On each side of the hall, there was a room connected to the hallway by matching sets of double doors. At the very end of the hallway, there was a kitchen and larder.

The old house continued to entice the children, despite stern lectures from Miss McCue and dire warnings from their parents. It wasn't long before three fifth grade boys became brave enough to push open the front door and peer inside. All it took was one dare after another, followed by a double dare or two, and the trio was well on their way to bragging rights about having been inside the old house. One afternoon, the three boys, Kip, Willie and James, decided it was time to investigate the old house once and for all. They agreed they would first search the rooms downstairs, and then, they would all go upstairs and see for themselves the room where the old witch had died. Being good Boy Scouts, they each went to school that day prepared, with a folding scout knife and a flashlight. The boys had told their mothers they were staying after school for extra help with their math (everyone knew how difficult long division with decimals could be). When the dismissal bell rang, the trio headed straight for the old house.

It was a dreary day; gray clouds covered the sky, and the air was still and cold. When they got to the front door, they glanced around to be sure no one was watching. Kip leaned against the heavy door, and it swung open with a great creak. Willie stepped inside and glanced around. Before he could take another step, Kip and James piled in behind him, bumping him from behind and sending the trio sprawling against the side wall. Just then, the front door slammed shut with a loud bang. The boys scrambled to their feet. They looked at one another wide eyed, each accusing the other of slamming the door. Willie, who was a bit taller and, therefore, considered himself the leader, turned on his flashlight and led the others farther down the hallway. It was a wide entrance with an old patterned tile floor. They used their flashlights to trace the cobwebbed molding across the high ceiling and illuminate each corner of the room, one by one.

Finally, they stood at the bottom of the old wooden stairs and aimed their lights on the dusty steps that led to the second floor. "Come on," Willie urged as he led them into the room to the right of the stairs. He pushed open the set of double doors that led into the room. It might have once been a dining room, but it was hard to tell. There wasn't much furniture, but the room was filled with clutter of all kinds. A light dangled from the ceiling on a lone wire. There were bags and cardboard boxes overflowing with what looked like old clothes, stacks of yellowed magazines and a bunch of very dusty and old stuffed animals. Most were missing their eyes, and the boys agreed that they smelled like old socks.

Coughing and mumbling, the boys followed Willie across the hall into the other room. This looked more like a living room, as there were some old pieces of furniture stacked up against a dusty and cluttered fireplace mantel. The boys flashed their lights across the room and into each corner. Everywhere they looked, it was the same—more boxes, bags, magazines and eyeless stuffed animals and dolls.

Just then, the patter of footsteps overhead stopped the boys dead in their tracks. They stood motionless, staring at one another. Willie put his finger to his lips to say, "Be quiet." Again, the footsteps echoed just above their heads. The footsteps stopped, but in their place, the wind began to beat on the sides of the house with the intensity of a hurricane. James mumbled under his breath, "What is that?" Willie peered out the front window onto Front Street. The trees were standing perfectly straight; there was not even a breeze flapping the leaves. Yet, the howling wind continued.

They quickly returned to the center hallway and stood at the bottom of the narrow wooden stairs staring at one another. "Let's go," Willie commanded as he charged up the stairs. With each step, the staircase creaked and groaned. Kip followed close behind, holding tightly to the dusty bannister. Close on his heels came James, who gingerly stepped on each tread. "Look, a footprint!" he gasped.

The other two laughed, "You jerk, those are our footprints!"

James took a deep breath, muttering to himself, "Oh, yeah."

Without warning, a cold wind swept down the staircase, engulfing the boys in an icy mist. They instantly began shivering. Then, the doors to the downstairs rooms slammed shut with a loud boom. With that, James leapt from the stairs and landed on the floor just inside the front door. He pulled on the latch and was out on the porch before Willie or Kip could respond. Kip and Willie looked at one another. Then, Willie called out, "Cluck, cluck, cluck! James is a chicken, cluck, cluck, cluck." At that moment, the front door once again slammed shut, and a booming laughter echoed through the house.

The two boys stood frozen about halfway up the stairs. It was then that the wind died down; in fact, it stopped howling altogether. As they moved up another step along the staircase, Kip's eyes grew wide; the wall along the staircase seemed to fill with air and expand. Just when the boys thought the wall would burst, there was an audible exhale, and the wall shrank back to normal.

"I'm out of here!" Kip yelped as he stumbled back down the stairs. He jerked on the front doorknob. For a long moment, it did not move. Then, ever so slowly, the great door swung open. Kip dashed through the opening to the safety of the porch.

Willie was left alone in the old house. He was nearly at the top of the stairs. Should he escape with the others or take a few more steps and see what was in the bedroom? The only sound he heard was the rattle of labored breathing coming from the nearby wall. He reached the landing, and as he turned to his right, every door in the house slammed open and shut again—except for the bedroom door that Willie was facing. Laughter echoed throughout the building, as the bedroom door swung open. Willie walked inside.

No one knows exactly what happened to Willie that day in the deserted bedroom in the old house. When he ran out the front door a few minutes later, his eyes were wide, sweat poured down his face and tears dribbled down his cheeks. When asked what happened, he could only stutter, "It—it—it." Willie never spoke of the old house to anyone again, not even his two best friends. And although Willie had never stammered before that day, he continues to do so to this very day.

MEET THE CRISIS SPECTERS

This type of ghost usually makes a one-time visit when an individual is under great emotional stress. During this appearance, the spirit may be coming to say goodbye or to offer comfort to a loved one. In some cases, one might see the apparition of a loved one at a very specific time of

day, such as precisely noon. The image suddenly disappears, and one may learn later that the friend had died at that exact hour. Other times, the crisis ghost appears when one is near to death. The spirit may be a sibling, parent or other loved one who arrives to help the person cross over. These apparitions are frequently observed during traumatic situations, such as combat, surgery, horrific accidents, grisly murders and terrorist attacks. They seldom appear more than three days after the individual's death.

The crisis specter is often associated with the guardian angel. *From www.freerangestock.com.*

A SISTERLY SPECTER IN RUMSON

A longtime Rumson resident who we will call Linda recently experienced a visit from a crisis ghost. Linda and her twin sister, Louise, were inseparable since their birth. As was the custom in those days, their mother dressed them in identical pink bonnets and playsuits. Eventually, they also wore matching sneakers, prom dresses and wedding gowns. Strangely, the girls never seemed to argue; they were always one another's very best friend. They shared a small pink and yellow bedroom, clothes, makeup and, once or twice, boyfriends.

Eventually, they were both married, and they lived just two blocks from one another in the same local town. Linda and Louise spoke several times each day, even if it was just a five-minute chat. Their children were more like brothers and sisters than cousins. Above all, the two sisters trusted one another explicitly. They shared their innermost secrets, and their hopes and dreams were a constant topic of conversation. They were such a pair that their teenage children laughingly called them the "pigeon sisters," after the characters in an episode of *The Odd Couple*.

One day Linda gave her sister the usual morning phone call. There was no answer. Although she thought it was strange at the time, Linda considered that perhaps Louise was still in the shower. She waited half an hour and called again, but there was still no answer. An uneasiness arose in Linda's chest—something wasn't right. She tried one more time, but the phone rang endlessly. She dumped her coffee down the sink, grabbed her jacket and keys and dashed out the door. Linda usually walked to Louise's house, but something was different about this morning. She jumped into her car and sped around the two blocks. She smiled to herself thinking about how Louise would tease her about driving over instead of taking the four-minute walk. When she pulled into the driveway, she saw that Linda's car was still in the garage. The door was locked. She tapped on the door and called out to her sister, "Hey, Lou, it's me!" When she got no response, she untangled Louise's house key from her key ring and opened the door.

That is when she found her. Louise was lying in a great heap in the kitchen as if she had simply melted onto the floor. The next days became a blur; decisions were made, services were attended and children were comforted. They were the worst days Linda had ever known. Without her sister, Linda found it difficult to face each day. She often found herself feeling angry whenever she heard people laughing. As time passed, Linda grew more and more depressed. She had difficulty carrying out daily tasks, and sometimes, just being awake was too painful.

One gray and rainy morning, Linda sat up in bed, drinking a cup of black coffee. She reached for the remote control for the television and ended the mindless chatter of the morning talk shows. Her eyes came to rest on an old photo on her nightstand. It was the two sisters, both pregnant at the time, posing in front of an old aluminum Christmas tree. As she smiled sadly at the photo, her trickle of tears became a deluge. Her guttural sobs seemed to ricochet off the bedroom walls as she laid her head back against the pillow. Something pulled her gaze toward the bedroom door. For an instant, the world stood still; there in the doorway stood Louise. She appeared exactly as she had the last time Linda had seen her alive, in her jogging suit and sneakers. She looked at Linda and smiled lovingly. Linda gasped and leapt from the bed with her arms outstretched. Before she could reach the doorway, her sister held up her hand to stop her. She never stopped smiling, but she slowly shook her head. "No, not yet," she whispered. In the next instant, she disappeared.

This was the only time Louise ever came to visit Linda. Louise knew that on that day, her sister desperately needed her comfort. Linda is still saddened by the loss of her sister, but now, she understands. Someday, the twins will be united again.

MEET THE RESIDUAL GHOSTS

Residual ghosts are some of the most common paranormal events reported. This spirit lives out its last few hours on this earth over and over again in endless agony. It is like a great picture loop that repeats without end. These specters do not seem to have consciousness or intelligence, nor can they interact or alter their pattern. An eighteenth-century residual apparition may appear repeatedly, with full period attire, hairstyle, mannerisms, décor and even foods evident. Such hauntings may be traumatic in nature, or they may simply be meaningful events from their life.

Closely related spirits are mental imprints. This residual tends to focus on one particular event, like an accident, murder, execution or some other traumatic scene. The incident itself is the apparition. They likely occur on very specific dates and precise times of day. Others are associated with a historic event, such as a war, depression or famine. In general, this form of apparition is believed to fade over time.

Another aspect of a residual haunting is the traditional ghost. Traditional ghosts are earthbound spirits that remain in one location.

The residual ghost is a location-centered spirit that seems to lack consciousness. *From www. common.wikimedia.net.*

These locations might be a historic building or a setting that was very important to a person in life. Although these hauntings go on for many years, they do not interact with humans. Such apparitions appear as solid beings that walk and act naturally.

APPARITION OF A TRAITOR: A PHANTOM STALKS NAVESINK

Another residual haunting from the days of the Revolutionary War is well known on the peninsula. This ghost, the specter of General Charles Lee, haunts the tip of the Highlands. Each night, the specter moves back and forth between two different lookout sites as if he can't decide which is the correct one to use. He scans the waters of the bay in search of something—or someone. The specter wears a dirty and disheveled Revolutionary War general's uniform, which has been stripped of its buttons, insignias and medals. He appears to be muttering or cursing, although no sound is ever heard.

Charles Lee, a former British military leader, moved to Virginia in 1773. When the Revolution started, Lee resigned his commission in the British army and offered his services to the Continental Congress. With such extensive experience, the Patriots gladly accepted his offer. General Lee fully expected to be named commander in chief, a job that went to George Washington. Lee quickly became known as an indecisive general who frequently ignored direct orders and made decisions that were not in the interest of the Patriot cause. On several occasions, he slowed down troop movements when ordered to expedite or retreated when told to advance. In addition, he maintained a constant stream of correspondence with the Continental Congress to complain about Washington. The matter came to a head when he failed to advance under a direct order from Washington at the Battle of Monmouth. Lee was stripped of command and was eventually court-martialed. His political connections within the Continental Congress resulted in the decision that there was insufficient evidence to condemn him to death. He retired to Virginia and died of a fever in Philadelphia in 1882.

Interestingly, documents found in 1885 verified that Lee was indeed in collusion with the British and that, while serving as a general in the Continental army, he was indeed a spy and a traitor. We can only assume that the apparition of General Charles Lee is spending eternity pacing the hilltops of the Navesink Highlands, still waiting for his British comrades to rescue him.

Meet the Ghosts Who Cannot Cross Over

There are those who say that all ghosts are those who have, for some reason, refused to or are unable to cross over to the next dimension. There appears to be multiple reasons why this occurs. Some spirits are afraid to move on; they don't seem to understand what has happened to them, and they may be afraid of leaving everything they know here on earth.

Spirits who do not realize they are dead do not cross over; they go on as if they are still alive. The classic example of this kind of haunting occurs when an older person who has lived in a residence for many years passes away. Unfortunately, the spirit does not realize they are dead, and they continue residing in the house as they did while they were alive. When a new owner moves into the house, the ghost sees these humans as invaders, resulting in some very stressful hauntings.

Ghost children also often fall into this category. In general, ghost children have been wrenched from life prematurely and don't understand where they are. They likely do not realize they are dead and are confused by their environment. They are lonely little souls that may be trapped where they died. Their deaths were most likely the results of horrific accidents,

The spirits of children often have difficulty crossing over. *From www.publicdomainpictures.net.*

terrifying violence or long, painful illnesses. These lonely spirits tend to be exceptionally sad and needy.

Likewise, ghosts with unfinished business often fail to cross over. There is something they didn't finish before death—something so important that they cannot or will not leave until the task is completed. In some cases, the spirit just wants to keep up with their family to ensure that they are okay; perhaps a mother's spirit stays to look over her children. Other ghosts have less altruistic motives. A specter who was murdered or tortured may seek vengeance on the person or family of the person who was responsible. They can be difficult spirits to convince to cross over, as they are never really satisfied.

AHCHINTAK

Navarumsunk's Persistent Phantom

In one such case, Ahchintak, a Lenape brave, has been unable to cross over for nearly 250 years. He lived on the peninsula with his tribe until 1755, when the government forced the Lenape into a deceitful land-for-nonviolence deal. It required the tribe to relocate to a settlement area in Burlington County. The settlement compelled the natives to adapt to a European lifestyle. The move was a failure; within a few years, the tribe moved to upper New York state to join other Native American tribes. Ahchintak, however, would have none of that. He simply refused to leave his home on the Navarumsunk Peninsula.

He had carried the name Ahchintak with him into adulthood; his stubbornness had been evident since he was a child. He was not very sociable with his tribe and certainly not with any of the settlers he encountered. He lived alone with his wife, who bore the brunt of his dreadful temper. It was not uncommon for him to defy the common decisions of the tribe, so no one was surprised when he simply refused to leave with them for Burlington County. He remained at the encampment with his wife and continued his antagonistic relationship with his settler neighbors.

Shortly after the tribe settled, they got word that Ahchintak was behaving aggressively toward the settlers on the peninsula. They feared that his behavior would endanger the nonviolence agreement the tribe had established with the settlers. An emissary was sent to convince Ahchintak to join the tribe in the new settlement. He was never heard from again. When he failed to return, another messenger was sent. He, too, disappeared without a trace. Later, Ahchintak boldly admitted that he had killed them for entering his property. Shortly afterward, the settlers tried to intervene when Ahchintak was caught beating his wife. When they rescued the bruised and bleeding woman, she explained that she had merely suggested that she wanted to go live with the remainder of the tribe. That very night, Ahchintak drowned his wife in a horse trough and left her body in the center of the settlers' village.

Ahchintak remained on his tiny tract of land for some years until he died. In fact, it seems that he never left at all. Soon afterward, the apparition of the vengeful brave, bloody tomahawk in hand, was first seen roaming the paths and roads of the peninsula, searching for something—or perhaps someone. Accounts of the sighting have continued over the years, with occasional sightings even today.

The ghost of Ahchintak is a force to be reckoned with. He is a towering, muscular image in full native dress. He wears worn moccasins, deerskin leggings and a long deerskin tunic. A thin rawhide headband from which two inverted feathers hang down his back encircles his head. His face is set in an earnest search. His dark eyes dart back and forth as he searches for invisible enemies or potential prey. His face is crunched into a scowl, and he breathes heavily, spewing a low guttural growling sound. It seems that Ahchintak's need for revenge has prevented his spirit from crossing over to a more peaceful existence. This need for revenge seems to power this negative phantom, forcing him to remain in this sphere, where his time has long since passed.

MEET THE GHOSTS OF ANIMALS AND OBJECTS

Ghostly encounters associated with non-living objects and animals are unique types of spirits. Throughout the centuries, history has recorded sightings of spiritually possessed inanimate objects. These objects can be anything from a child's toy or doll to a train or even a ship. They can also be a mother's favorite photograph of her infant or Grandfather's favorite shotgun. They may not be rare or expensive items; they could be something as inane as a cowboy hat, a favorite book or even a broken clock. Sometimes, these objects take on characteristics of residuals and

Apparitions of beloved pets are common among bereaved pet owners. *From www.pixabay.com.*

simply repeat a specific behavior over and over in a never-ending cycle. Other times, these objects may behave more like intelligent spirits and appear to interact with the living.

Many authors have concluded that these possessed objects may be culturally sensitive. In Great Britain, it is believed that weapons and jewelry are the objects that are most likely to be haunted, while in America, toys and dolls seem to carry this distinction. Many world cultures hold that ritual memorabilia, artifacts and religious keepsakes and relics are most likely to exhibit supernatural powers.

In cultures where animals are kept as pets, there is considerable discussion about the possibility of an afterlife for these beloved animals. There is a huge debate over whether animals have souls or not. An equal number of pet owners believe, without a doubt, that their beloved pets do have souls and that they will be reunited with their pets in the afterlife. Spiritual literature is full of accounts of apparitions, manifestations and other paranormal evidence that beloved pets have lingered after death and have spiritually

Haunted objects can be as small as a piece of jewelry or large as a house. *From www. freeimages.com.*

interacted with their masters. Animal phantoms are found most frequently in situations where the human and animal spent long periods of time in stressful or dangerous situations. This is true of soldiers and their military dogs and policemen and their canines—not to mention seeing eye dogs or emotional support animals. An account shared by a longtime Fair Haven resident testifies to this phenomenon.

ARNOLD'S DAILY DUTY

A Fair Haven Phantom

Back in the days of the paddle-wheelers, the little village of Fair Haven woke early, as the sound of the steam whistles echoed up and down the Navesink. Like a gust from a nor'easter, the sound of ships' airhorns ricocheted along the single-lane streets that lay perpendicular to the river. The sound woke the village, telling them another day had begun. For Arnold, it was the signal that it was time to get to work.

Arnold had many responsibilities. One of his many tasks was to greet the steamships as they docked in Fair Haven. He could hear ships coming while they were still upriver, and he always managed to be waiting at the pier when they docked. He waited patiently to see who alighted from the boats and watched apprehensively as locals strolled up the gangways for their daily trip into the city. After the ships departed, Arnold would trot back to DeNormandie Avenue and resume his usual routine.

Arnold spent the rest of the morning visiting his neighbors on the street, one after another. He checked to see who was cooking, cleaning or getting ready for work. He wandered across lawns, checked out new flower beds and sat beneath the forsythia in time to watch the children meander up the street toward the school. Usually, someone offered him a morning snack, and if he played his cards right, he could find lunch farther down the lane. And there was always a treat here and there wherever he showed up. When school let out, Arnold was on his post, greeting the kids with a wagging tail and jostling with them as they ran home to change into their play clothes.

Yes, Arnold was a dog. He officially lived on DeNormandie Avenue but considered the adjacent streets his territory as well. He deemed the families on the street his family and the kids on the street his kids. In addition to meeting the steamboats, Arnold kept watch over the children on the street. A crying baby or the wail of a youngster with a skinned knee would bring Arnold running. He also kept a close eye on strangers who walked the street. Whenever the kids went exploring or went down to the river, Arnold went, too. Sometimes, he just sat on the little sandy beach area and watched; other times, he joined in on the fun and came home just like the kids, soaked to the bone and covered in sand.

Everyone agreed that Arnold was a handsome rascal. He was part Labrador retriever and part who knows what. The tips of his ears were a bold copper hue, while his coat was a rich fawn color, with spurts of white around his face, chest and paws. As Arnold grew older, the white hair around his muzzle intensified, and the tips of his ears also took on a whiteish hue. One spring, people noticed that Arnold, who was then called Old Arnold, had slowed down. He no longer raced across lawns to meet the steamboats; rather, he trotted at a leisurely pace in a nonchalant manner. He maintained his daily rounds but was less likely to visit the entire street before noon. He was often seen sleeping beneath the forsythia bush or stretched out on one of Mrs. Smith's chaise longue chairs. He still tried to keep up with the kids, but it was more difficult, so he usually just sat and watched the fun instead of joining in his favorite game of keep away.

Then, one morning, Arnold could not be found. No one met the steamboat that morning, and there was no one to watch the children as they headed up the street to school. They found him later, lying beneath the forsythia bush. Arnold had passed away. Sadness surrounded the street for several days. Everyone talked about what a wonderful dog Arnold had been. His master buried him there beneath the forsythia because it was his favorite place. At first, children brought bouquets of dandelion flowers for his grave, but the grass eventually grew over his plot, and by the summertime, people had stopped talking about Arnold altogether.

The Fourth of July was on a Saturday that year, and the entire town geared up for a busy and exciting weekend. There would be boat rides, fishing, swimming, picnics and backyard clambakes. On the eve of the holiday, the temperatures soared into the high nineties. Windows were opened wide; kids ran about in their swimsuits and the older folks tried to keep cool by sitting under shade trees with cool drinks. By midafternoon, most of the children were down at the river. Some waded at the water's edge, others splashed one another in water up to their waists. Three or four boys tossed a ball back and forth over an imaginary net, while a few older kids were holding a swimming tournament, swimming laps between the shore and the outer boundary of the swim area, which was marked by a single white rope. Several mothers sat on the sand, chatting with one another. They periodically scanned the water, watching the kids at play.

The women had just gotten into a discussion about the best recipes for chowder when they noticed a commotion in the water several yards from shore. The children were all shouting and screaming, pointing toward the far side of the beach. The women soon joined in the screaming, as there, in the deeper water away from all the other swimmers, a small child in a reddish-orange swimsuit was flailing in the water. Little arms waved frantically in the air before suddenly disappearing. One woman raised her skirt to her knees and rushed into the surf, but she soon stumbled and fell into the water herself. Suddenly, a large fawn-colored dog darted across the beach and dove into the water. It paddled to the site where the child had disappeared. For a moment, no one could see the dog, but his head suddenly emerged from the water. In his teeth, he clutched the reddish-orange swimsuit. He started swimming toward shore with the small child dangling from his mouth. When he reached the beach, he dropped the child at the feet of the women.

Help seemed to come from everywhere, and soon, the child was whisked away. Everyone stood about chattering excitedly about what had just happened. It was several minutes before anyone thought to look for the dog that had rescued the child, but it was nowhere to be found. No one claimed to be its master, and no one remembered having seen the dog in the neighborhood. The adults were in a quandary over the identification of the dog. One person said it had no collar, but another insisted the collar was red. A witness declared that it was a fawn-colored dog, while someone else supposed it was more whitish-tan. An older boy insisted that it was probably a lab or maybe just a mutt. One man said that it had reddish ears, but that didn't help. No one could remember having ever seen the dog before. Then, a small voice broke through the chatter: "I know who the dog is!" He announced, "It's Old Arnold—I'd know him anywhere." A few of the adults laughed out loud at the child. Everyone knew that Old Arnold was dead. He had been gone for several months. Some smiled and patted the boy on his back, while others looked away and exchanged bewildered glances.

Later, as folks settled down for the night, they began to replay the day's events and considered the possibility that what the child had suggested was true. Eventually, most came to agree that it could have been none other than Old Arnold who came back from the grave to save one of his kids.

Meet the Living Ghosts and Photographic Specters

This unusual type of specter is also one of the most interesting. This manifestation occurs when the soul has left the body, but the individual is still alive. This can occur when an individual is very near death and the spirit leaves to say goodbye to a loved one. We usually associate the term with the projection of a living person, an identical copy that is seen by others or sometimes by the individual themselves. It may be the person at their true age or even as a child. In some instances, these spirits can

The living ghost manifests when a soul leaves before the moment of death. *From www. oldbookillustrations.com.*

even be your own projection that others can see but you cannot. In this instance, someone may claim to have seen you at a specific location at a very specific time, but you know you were nowhere near the site. The image is so perfect that they will likely argue with you about the appearance. These ghosts show both intelligence and self-awareness.

Occasionally, individuals see their own image, which is known as a doppelgänger. This is a word derived from the German *doppel*, which means double, and *gänger*, which means doer. Many doppelgängers foretell death. It is said that Abraham Lincoln saw his doppelgänger in a mirror on the morning before he was assassinated.

Unique photographic ghosts are usually recognized as a family member or friend. *From www. opensourceillustrations.com.*

Another peculiar specter is the photographic ghost. This spirit is not observed at the moment the photo is taken. Yet, once the photo is completed, the apparition is clearly visible. Sometimes, it appears as a cloudlike form; other times, it is a full-body, identifiable manifestation.

ONE LAST VISIT TO NANA'S HOUSE

For as long as Matthew could remember, he had spent his summers at the Jersey Shore. Long before he was born, his grandparents had purchased a rambling house just off Ocean Avenue in Monmouth Beach. The house was full of memories of carefree summer days, splashing in the ocean and digging clams along the river. Most of all, Matthew remembered Nana. He recalled her clambakes out in the backyard, being washed down with the garden hose when he came back from the beach and even Nana's elegant Christmas Eve dinners, where he often complained about the mandatory shirt and tie. The house was full of memories of Nana. They had moved to the beach permanently when Grandpa retired. And even after he died, Nana stayed. She always claimed it was her one true home, and she declared that she would never leave it. But Nana was gone, and it was time to put the house on the market.

Most of the family had scattered across the country, except for Matthew, who settled down in nearby Little Silver. It became his task to organize the distribution of her belongings. He decided to hold one last family reunion in the old house, and he even planned one of Nana's elegant dinners to say goodbye. On the appointed weekend, despite the cold weather, the family came back for one final visit to the beach. Soon, the house was filled with laughter and the clink of wine glasses. The long dining table was set with Nana's best china, silverware and linens. There was a fire roaring in the hearth, and on the mantel, there was a large framed photograph of the entire family that had been taken two years before on Nana's ninetieth birthday. They all stood together in their best attire (shirts and ties, of course) with Nana settled regally in her favorite wingback chair in the very center.

Everyone was in a fine mood, chatting and laughing and sharing the latest family news with one another. Soon, they were recounting stories from their days at the beach. The subject always came back to Nana and her firm but loving manner. Nana was indeed a woman to be reckoned with. She was the matriarch of the family; she knew it and lived accordingly. They laughed about the times they tried to tell Nana a fib and how they were never successful. They chuckled over the great debates they used to have about planning an event, knowing it was Nana who made the final decision.

They finished dinner and were waiting for the forty-five minutes Nana always insisted must pass before dessert was served. Matthew pulled out his camera and suggested they have one last family photo taken in the old house. There were a couple of good-natured snipes about Matthew and his love of photography, but everyone agreed it was a good idea. While the family jockeyed for position in front of the fireplace, Matthew set up the tripod and double-checked his remote control. Everyone was there for this one last photograph—everyone except Nana. It took several attempts, as people laughed at the wrong time and the toddlers wandered away. Finally, the camera clicked, and someone shouted, "It's a take!" The family scurried back to their spots on the sofas and chairs that surrounded the great hearth.

When Matthew checked the images, he couldn't believe his eyes. There in the photograph was the family smiling back at the camera. In the exact center of the photograph, Nana was regally posed in her favorite wingback chair. It was a full-body apparition, somewhat grayish in color. Obviously, Nana was not about to miss this last family photograph.

For as long as such records have been kept, the two rivers region has been blessed or cursed (you choose the word) with countless ghostly and supernatural encounters. These descriptions are just a few of the accounts of the apparitions, specters and singularly peculiar events that have occurred and continue to occur here in the land between the two rivers.

2
THE GHOSTLY SPIRIT
OF THE *MARY & ME*

A TALE OF PROHIBITION

On January 17, 1920, the news flashed across the nation as countless headlines proclaimed the beginning of Prohibition in the United States. On that day, the Eighteenth Amendment to the Constitution went into effect. It forbade the manufacture, sale or transport of intoxicating liquors within the United States. The act did not prohibit the consumption of alcohol, but it banned its production and distribution by both private and commercial means, so it had the same effect. This was the first day of what became thirteen years of civil disobedience and internal turmoil across the nation. It came complete with moonshine stills, clandestine breweries, bootlegging, fraudulent medical practices, smuggling, hidden speakeasies, corruption and even murder. To many locals of the Jersey Shore, it was more like a second Civil War.

While the effect of Prohibition nationwide was significant, the effect on the day-to-day life of local shore residents was tumultuous. Practically overnight, bootlegging in the form of "rumrunning" became a local and, sometimes, community industry. Since the legislation was not particularly popular in the area to begin with, it took little encouragement to persuade locals to participate in the budding rumrunning business. Both professional and recreational fishermen, and frankly anyone with a boat, promptly became one of the well-known "rumrunners of the Jersey Shore."

This form of bootlegging sprung up all along the New Jersey coast. Yet, it was on the eastern Monmouth County shoreline and along the banks of the twin rivers, the Navesink and Shrewsbury, that rumrunning became an enormous, although illegal, industry. The ragged coastline, with its many modest inlets, secluded coves and winding creeks, was an asset to the local bootleggers. Access to the ocean enabled smugglers to operate with relative ease, and the area's proximity to the dense populations of New York, Philadelphia, Washington and Baltimore provided a market. It is said that one could easily deduce when a fisherman began rumrunning because his family started to eat better, and his bills got paid.

Originally, the U.S. territorial limit from the coast was three nautical miles. It was just beyond this site that the famous "Rum Row" formed. Dozens of large freighters stocked with liquor from Europe, Canada, Bermuda and the Caribbean jockeyed for position. As the ships were in international waters, the government was unable to prevent the flotilla of ships from anchoring. These large crafts, called motherships, remained in place for months at a time, serving as floating warehouses. Freighters from around the world supplied the motherships daily with renewed cargo of whiskey, scotch, gin, vodka, bourbon and rye. When the sun set, the fleet of local rumrunners raced to the motherships and offloaded the precious cargo.

For hometown rumrunners, often referred to as "rummers," it was a quick trip out to the waiting freighters. Under the cover of darkness and with a bit of luck, they quickly loaded their small crafts and raced for the shore to a secluded dock on one of the two sister rivers. There, they could offload their cargo and collect their fee. Even a small boat could make the equivalent of $150 in today's money per trip. A rummer could make two trips a night if they were lucky. Sources say thirty-five thousand cases of liquor were smuggled each night along the New Jersey Shore.

Many of the rummers were revealed to be true entrepreneurs. These boatmen didn't approach freighters empty-handed. They came with groceries, vegetables, mail, baked goods, warm clothing, newspapers and even fresh water. They sold these goods to the crew members of the motherships and often carried messages and mail back to the mainland. Locals tried to camouflage their boats by painting each side different colors, adding or removing fishing gear and even repainting the nameplate on the stern daily with a different name. It was serious business for rummers. If they were caught by the coast guard, both their cargo and boat would be confiscated.

It wasn't long before organized crime realized the tremendous profits involved in smuggling and began taking over the business, so the local runners had two foes. They not only had to worry about the federal agents, but they now faced a band of gangsters equipped with both high-speed boats and heavy-duty arms. When a rum war broke out between the crime families, the local rumrunners were caught in the middle. Soon, a legion of gangsters was focused on driving the locals out of the rumrunning business.

Organized criminals attacked local rummers, killed their crews, burned their crafts and terrorized their families and friends. The corruption of local leaders was blatant, and actual warfare broke out in local waters and along the shoreline. As hard times returned to the local fishermen, a series of peculiar, unexplainable and even paranormal events arose.

The folklore of this area during Prohibition is bursting with accounts of strange apparitions, unexplained phenomena and just plain creepy happenings. One such tale takes place in the backwaters of the Shrewsbury River, where the estuary begins to widen into an almost lake-like appearance. There, the irregular coastline is dotted with an assortment of small coves, creeks, inlets and countless tidal pools. All along the shoreline, hidden among the seagrass and Phragmites, small docks cling onto the marsh.

Jessie had lived on the Shrewsbury his entire life. Just like his father before him, he was a fisherman. He always knew he would become a fisherman long before he bought his first boat, the *Mary & Me*. He worked the rivers and bay for ten to twelve hours a day, fishing and clamming, trying to feed his growing family. He lived with his wife and three children in a small ramshackle cottage in the small fishing community that was once known as Galilee. Jessie had lived on the water for as long as he could remember. He had learned to swim before he could walk and knew the names of every marine plant and animal found along the riverbanks. He not only understood the tide cycle as well as he knew his own name, but he could identify the exact location of the Shrewsbury's many hidden shoals that may have endangered his boat.

When Prohibition was young, Jessie quickly realized he could supplement his meager income by doing a bit of rumrunning. It wasn't complicated. Each night, after dark, he simply motored the *Mary & Me* down the Shrewsbury, along the barrier island. He proceeded past the mouth of the Navesink, where the two rivers meet. From there, it was a short run to the bay. After skirting Sandy Hook, he would race out to meet a freighter on Rum Row. He quickly picked up his cargo of illegal liquor and retraced his path as rapidly and unobtrusively as possible. He delivered his cargo to a designated dock on the Shrewsbury and was soon home, safe and sound. Those times were good for Jess and his family. He put food on the table, the kids no longer wore hand-me-downs and the worried look on his wife's face vanished. Although he never said it aloud, Prohibition was the best thing that had ever happened to him.

Then, gangsters from the organized crime families began taking over the rumrunning business. It quickly became a dangerous endeavor. Two of Jessie's friends were murdered, and at least three fellow fishermen had simply disappeared during rum runs. He and the *Mary & Me* had been chased and even shot at once. But after that last night on the river, the night he abandoned the *Mary & Me*, and just seconds before it exploded into a fiery ball of flames, Jessie gave up bootlegging for good.

With the loss of his boat and the serious injuries he sustained from the incident, Jessie once again faced a meager existence. Once again, he knew the feeling of want and fear that he could not provide for his family. In the coming days and weeks, Jessie's body healed as much as it ever would. He walked with a limp from the fractures and burns he suffered that night. Weakness in his legs and back prevented him from fishing anymore, so he began knitting nets for the other fishermen, and he made just enough to keep food on the table.

On a particularly cool autumn night, ten long years later, Jessie limped across the small plank platform that served as a porch. Using his cane to support his weight, he eased himself onto the top step and leaned against the worn four-by-four that he used as a porch post. As he sat staring across the river, he instinctively reached into his windbreaker for his pipe. But then he remembered he had no tobacco. There had been no tobacco for a very long time.

As he so often did, Jessie began thinking about the *Mary & Me*, and he tried to remember when he first saw the apparition. He had witnessed the specter for so many years now, but it was no use; he couldn't remember the first time he saw it. Others had seen it before him, and it became the local chinwag for a while. Even his wife saw it before he did. One day, years ago, Mary had charged into the cottage shrieking nonsensibly. She had seen the apparition of the *Mary & Me*, fully engulfed in flames, floating toward the shore in front of their house. Sometime later, Jessie began seeing it too.

At first, he only saw it every once in a while, when the weather was cold and overcast like it was on that last night. Then, it began to appear more and more often. It was always the same. He saw his beloved *Mary & Me* floating aimlessly down the Shrewsbury, with its pilothouse surrounded by huge flames. As he watched, the boat began curving toward the shore. There was a moment when it seemed to stop dead in the water; then, a loud boom echoed across the river as the sky filled with millions of fiery fragments of the *Mary & Me*. Although he felt the heat from the explosion, his body stayed icy cold. Then, he began to see it often—always at night, regardless of the weather. It always seemed to appear when the household kitty was nearly empty, but then, that was most of the time these days.

It had been his first real fishing boat, and he loved *Mary & Me* almost as much as he loved Mary, his wife. Local rumormongers and tattlers claimed the apparition was an evil omen. Although it broke his heart each time he watched it explode into millions of pieces, he began to look forward to the apparition. For some inexplicable reason, it reassured him of something he couldn't quite explain. And every time, he relived that final and unforgettable night.

Jessie sat on the steps until darkness spread across the river like an endless black shroud. Before his eyes, the *Mary & Me* emerged from the marsh, fully ablaze. In an instant, he was taken back to that night. It was a cold, windy day; the sky was overcast, and bad weather threatened. The river was a muddy brown, swirling away from the tide that shoved the Phragmites against the shoreline. Along the sandy berm, the marsh gave way to a layer of packed snow. Jessie shouted goodbye as he slammed the front door against the icy wind with one hand and balanced a basket of fresh-baked bread and cakes in the other. He hurried toward the *Mary & Me*, which sat gently rocking at the dock. Although it wasn't far to the river, the wind was so bitter that he pulled his ear flaps down around his head as he walked.

When Jessie reached the *Mary & Me*, he couldn't help himself; he smiled. It was a handsome craft—perhaps not to others, but Jessie thought it to be beautiful. It was a worthy vessel, with a small pilothouse and a deep, flat floor that had carried many a full load of fish over the years. These days, it was also doing a regular nighttime rum run, but it didn't seem to mind the extra work. It had survived many a nor'easter, a few chases by the coast guard and even one or two tussles with the gangsters. As he prepared for the nightly run, Jessie remembered how shiny and white the boat used to look. Now that he was running rum, he was forced to paint it different colors every few weeks in hopes of camouflaging it from the coast guard. Even the boat's name plate had been switched many times. *Coral Lady*, *Sweet Surprise* and *Fish's Foe* were only a few of the names it had sported across its stern. But to Jessie, it was always the *Mary & Me*.

By early evening, he had collected and packed his "trading items" into baskets and carefully tucked them into the pilothouse. In addition to the fresh-baked goods—compliments of Mary—he had newspapers, tobacco, some vegetables and several cans of coffee. He hastily wrote a price on the outside of the basket. He planned to sell these to the foreman on the freighter for a bit of extra cash. He liked to call that his private stash, and he used it to buy treats for his kids and a little something for his beloved wife, Mary.

This last run started out like any other. He always left the dock well after dark, and he always had a full load of fuel. He headed along the Shrewsbury, like all the other boats, looking like he was on his way out for a night of fishing off the coast. He watched the lights in Sea Bright as they glistened off his starboard, and he soon caught a glimpse of the Highlands lights ahead. Soon, he was in the bay, moving toward the tip of Sandy Hook. The water was a bit choppier there than it had been in the river, but Jessie didn't mind; he focused on the course ahead. He wasn't alone on the water that night, as there seemed to be an armada of fishermen headed out to the deep water.

Jessie kept as close to Sandy Hook as he dared. Once he passed the tip, he headed east-southeast, hoping to avoid confrontation with either the coast guard or the gangsters. This added some time to the trip, but it was safer this way. As he navigated into the darkness, Jessie checked his compass repeatedly. In the distance, he could make out a thin row of lights. Jessie shivered and adjusted the woolen hat farther down on his head. Despite the bitter cold on the open ocean, he was in good spirits. After this run, he planned to take a few days off to do some repair work on the cottage and spend time with Mary and the kids.

The ocean was relatively calm, and there seemed to be little traffic on the route. He saw only a few other boats heading in his direction. To anyone else, they looked like regular fishermen, but Jessie knew them to be fellow rummers. As he approached the territorial limits, he could see the mothership, a giant freighter loaded with illegal liquor, bobbing gently in the waves. He checked his compass and chart once more, making certain he was safely within international waters before he turned on his running lights. Using a small lantern, he flashed the signal to the freighter. For a few moments, there was no response. Then, he saw it—the quick double flash from the mothership. It was safe to proceed.

As he approached, he wondered what it was like to be aboard the mothership for weeks and months at a time, with no news, no mail, no Mary or the kids. As he pulled beside the mothership, giant ropes fell from the deck, which Jessie quickly attached to both the bow and stern of his boat. The crew foreman peered down from above. Jessie immediately held up his large basket as high as he could. A reply from the deck, "Good man!" Another long rope was immediately dropped into the boat, which Jessie quickly attached to the basket. In one quick motion, the basket was hoisted onto the deck.

At the same time, two crewmen from the freighter scampered down a rope ladder and joined Jessie on the deck of the *Mary & Me*. An enormous wench on the stern of the freighter whirled into action, extending a long steel arm over the side of the freighter, just above Jessie's boat. Attached to the steel cable was a hefty cargo net filled with dozens of barrels of Irish whiskey. As soon as it was within reach, the two-man crew began hoisting the barrels aboard the *Mary & Me*. Jessie directed the loading to ensure that it would not shift during the trip back upriver. When the net was empty, a crewman flashed a signal, and the net was whisked back aboard the freighter. Jessie and the crewmen quickly shook hands and wished one another good luck. By the time the crewmen had reached the top of the rope ladder, Jessie had unleashed himself from the mothership.

He checked to be certain his lights were doused and pulled away from the freighter. He eased away into the darkness, slowly at first, as not to call any attention to himself. Checking his watch, he realized he would be fighting the tide going home. That meant he couldn't travel as quickly as he would like, and with a full load, he would burn a lot more fuel.

When he was some distance away, he pushed the throttle forward and began the long, dark journey home. Jessie was fully alert, as this was the dangerous segment of the trip. In addition to the difficulty of navigating in the total darkness, he also had to keep a keen eye out for both the coast guard and the gangsters. If the coast guard caught him, they would arrest him, confiscate the cargo and, worst of all, seize or destroy the *Mary & Me*. Confronting the gangsters could prove to be even worse. They often traveled in packs, like wolves, and played by their own rules. They had no hesitation when robbing and killing anyone who they caught running rum.

The *Mary & Me* moved quickly but fervently toward the Highlands and the mouth of the two rivers. The air was frigid, and the ocean was a bit choppy, but Jessie paid little attention to it. He was focused on his path through the dark waters and was constantly scanning the surface on each side. His eyes strained to peer through the darkness in search of both the light-colored hulls of the coast guard and the dark, shadowy vessels that were more likely to be the gangsters. He breathed uneasily, darting his eyes to and fro searching as far as the horizon in every direction. As he neared the tip of Sandy Hook, he paused the boat for a moment to take a closer look at his surroundings. The route looked clear, so Jessie thrust the level forward, and the *Mary & Me* darted past Sandy Hook and into the bay. He didn't slow down, not even as he approached the mouth of the rivers.

Just as he passed under the Highlands Bridge, he saw something out of the corner of his eye. It was something small and dark on his starboard. He turned to look again; it was definitely moving. The hair on the back of his neck stood straight up. He strained his eyes to scour the darkness. It was a boat, and it was following him. The *Mary & Me* raced up the river. Jessie checked his instrument panel and winced; if only he wasn't fighting the tide. He just couldn't make the speed he wanted.

As he approached the small sedge islands at the mouth of the Navesink, he considered darting into the estuary and hiding among the scrub and reed beds. He thought better of it; he had to keep moving to disappear within the marshy cluster of islands in the Shrewsbury. Perhaps the Shrewsbury would be too shallow during this tide for the pursuit vessel. It was a treacherous run, and Jess knew it. He had to keep an eye on the dark vessel and avoid the countless shoals and small sedge islands that dotted the Shrewsbury. The boat was in high gear, pushing back against the current.

The *Mary & Me* had never reached this speed before; at times, it seemed to be lifting right out of the water. Jessie frowned when he heard a low moaning coming from the engine. Again, he looked at the vessel approaching him on his starboard. Each time he looked back, he saw it was coming closer and closer.

Suddenly, he heard another engine. For a second, he thought the noise was coming from the *Mary & Me*, but it was not. It was loud and close—too close to be coming from the boat in pursuit. This time, Jessie spun to look to port and gasped in shock. There, just a few yards off his stern, a black-hulled speed boat was closing in on him. To his horror, Jessie saw three men holding torches aboard the boat. He knew immediately what that meant. Although he was freezing cold, sweat ran down his face. He tried to swerve back and forth to prevent from being overtaken, but it was no use. There was a gunshot, and the dark vessel pulled beside. In an instant, a burning torch flew through the air and landed on the bow of the *Mary & Me*.

Jessie saw the flames leaping toward the pilothouse. He knew they would reach the cargo of whiskey within minutes. He couldn't leave the wheel to fight the fire, but he knew that, at any moment, all that alcohol would explode. He looked toward the shore and gave the wheel a hard pull to the right. The boat curved toward the marshland ahead. Jessie crawled over the barrels of whiskey to the stern. He crept up the washboard and, without pausing to glance back, dove into the frigid water. Just then, a huge fireball filled in the night sky over the Shrewsbury. Pieces of the *Mary & Me* fluttered down to the water's surface. Within seconds, the dark-hulled speed boat was racing back downstream.

The *Linwood*, a rumrunner's vessel, is alight after an encounter with gangsters. *From the U.S. Coast Guard, Image #193:5-4-23, 1923.*

Jessie didn't remember hitting the water or the initial searing burn from the explosion. He dove as deeply as he could, surfacing several yards away. When he came up for air, he sputtered and gasped in the bitter cold. His eyes failed to focus, and he could see only a fiery glow against the night sky. It was then that he realized his beloved boat was gone, but he was not aware that he was seriously injured. Just then, the searing pain hit him, and for a moment, he sank beneath the water. He couldn't remember how he managed to get to shore. The most he could recall was swimming—well, trying to swim. His left leg would not move, and there was a penetrating kind of pain that took his breath away. Somehow, he found himself on the berm of a soggy patch of marsh.

Jessie didn't know how long he had lain there, but when he awoke, it was daylight. He was covered with painful cuts and bruises, but they were nothing compared to the unyielding pain in his leg. He tried to sit up but flopped back on the sand. When he finally managed to get a look at his leg, all he could see was a bloody mass of charred skin and a ragged bone protruding from his pant leg. To that day, Jessie wondered how his neighbor had known to come over to the far side of the marsh to look for him; it was out of the way for sure. It really didn't matter, as he was rescued and taken ashore. There, he spent many painful months recovering from his broken bones and burned flesh.

Jessie rubbed the tender skin of his leg and used the cane to lift the weakened leg onto the step. As he looked out over the river, the wind picked up. At first, it was just a waft of air, but then, it became a steady wind. He felt the gust slap his face, and he smiled. The *Mary & Me* was coming again, and he knew it. That was unusual, as he had never seen the apparition twice in one night. As he looked across the marsh, a flicker of light appeared. Ever so slowly, the glow grew brighter until the manifestation of the ship, fully engulfed in flames, drifted toward the shore. Jessie didn't turn his eyes away as the burning specter approached. All he saw was the *Mary & Me* as it used to be, its shining white hull and polished wooden trim glistening on an ocean of blue. Jessie's smile grew into a broad grin. It was so beautiful. It had fed his family for many years and had always brought him safely home. Even on that last night, *Mary & Me* had given its all to bring him home.

It had been some time since Jessie had spoken of the apparition. For years, he had refused to discuss it, even with his wife. Locals who claimed to have seen it had been rebuffed when they tried to share their sightings. It was not until the old man died that night, sitting on his porch steps, that the apparition vanished and was never seen again.

3
THE HEARTLESS GHOST OF
PASSAGE POINT

I f you had met Lewis Morris, the royal governor of New Jersey in the
seventeenth century, your opinion of him would largely be determined
by the color of your skin. You see, Lewis Morris was born into a family
whose wealth was the result of owning enslaved people. In 1692, his uncle,
also known as Lewis, died, leaving him not only a prosperous ironworks
business in nearby Shrewsbury but also a large plantation in what is now
Rumson, New Jersey.

Consisting of more than eight hundred acres, Passage Point Plantation
was run by a staff of indentured European servants as well as at least seventy
slaves. The plantation's acreage included woodlands, farmland, a manor
house, a shoreline, a commercial loading dock, slave quarters and various
shops and work sheds.

The plantation provided agricultural produce for use in the ironworks
settlement and the markets in New York City. Packet ships docked daily
to pick up fresh produce, and they left behind goods for distribution
along the Jersey coast. The new master expanded the plantation and ran
his properties with an iron fist. Fellow landowners knew him to be self-
absorbed, serious and unpleasant. The enslaved people on his plantation
knew him to be harsh, unyielding and cruel. With each passing year, he
became more ruthless and vicious.

The lives of the slaves at Passage Point were arduous and demoralizing.
Morris devised more humiliating and cruel punishments for both real and
perceived misbehavior. He perfected punishment techniques that resulted

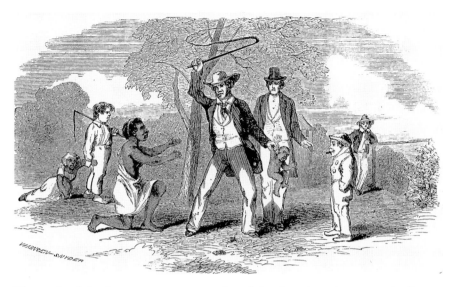

The cruelty of the slave owner was common knowledge throughout the community. *From www.commons.wikimedia.net.*

in the disfigurement of the accused. It was often quipped that the master was indeed heartless. He once executed an enslaved person who reported that one of the farm sheds was ablaze. Lewis declared the man to be guilty of arson, and the man was incinerated while locked in an outdoor toilet. In the summer of 1695, Morris called out to an elderly female slave who was working in the fields. When she did not respond, he walked up to her, put a gun to her head and pulled the trigger. We do not know if she ignored his instructions or if she even heard him. He forced the other women to take her body to the slave quarters, where he hung it from a tree for three days. Although the slaves attempted to get legal action against Morris, they were rebuffed by local authorities.

Morris appeared to be in a constant state of rage, as tensions grew throughout the remainder of that summer and fall. In October, seven enslaved people attempted to speak with Morris about his extreme cruelty and the death of the older enslaved woman. A scuffle ensued, and Morris was shot dead by a bullet through his heart. At such a close range, the heart itself was expelled.

The seven enslaved people were arrested and tried within a few hours. Two were acquitted; the others, including Oliver, Agbee and Jeremy, were found guilty. Although Agbee escaped, he was quickly recaptured. Oliver managed to obtain a lesser sentence; he was whipped so severely that he was totally disfigured. Agbee and Jeremy, who were believed to be the ringleaders, were sentenced to death. They were first tied to a post while their hands were sawed off. Bleeding and in agony, they were forced to watch as their hands were burned. Then, the two were taken and hanged until they were nearly dead. Finally, they were pulled down and burned alive. The ghastly execution was forcibly witnessed by the remainder of the enslaved people at the plantation.

Agbee, Jeremy and Oliver became heroes to the remaining slaves on the plantation. Stories of their bravery and courage to confront cruelty and prayers that they may rest in peace were passed down by word of mouth for countless years. By all accounts, they have done so.

The same cannot be said for their merciless master, Lewis Morris. For over the next one hundred years, reports circulated that an apparition of Morris was seen scouring Passage Plantation as if searching for something. The ghostly specter has a gaping hole in his chest that is so large one can see straight through it. For many years after his death, it was reported that the ghost would sometimes approach a field of workers and demand that they search for his heart.

Today, sightings of the phantom are sporadic, although they are rather more frequent during the month of October. Some say he still searches Passage Point for his missing heart. Occasionally, a resident will call the authorities about a suspicious-looking character combing the neighborhood as if in a desperate search for something. Can it be that the former royal governor, Lewis Morris, will forever search for his missing heart? He doesn't realize his search is in vain, for just as his slaves knew so many years ago, Lewis Morris was heartless in life. So, it is fitting that he is heartless in death.

4

CURSE OF THE CANIS LUPUS

One dark and windy night, just as Oliver William Holton, his wife and two young sons sat down to dinner in their new home, there was a loud, demanding knock on the front door. Annoyed at being disturbed at dinner, Mr. Holton clutched his dinner napkin with one hand as he jerked open the door with the other. An old woman was perched on his doorstep, leaning inward, trying to avoid the rain. "What do you want?" he demanded.

The woman stared silently into his face. She was frail, with olive, canvas-like skin. Her large brown eyes seemed too large for her face, and her expression was that of one who was weary but earnest in her efforts. Her hair was tightly braided, and a brightly colored shawl encased her face in vivid reds and blues. The remainder of her clothing was dark, ill-fitting and shabby. And if she was wearing shoes, they were mere scuffs hidden beneath her mud-caked hem.

"Well," Holton demanded, "what do you want?"

Never taking her eyes off his, she spoke in a low, hoarse voice, "I am here to help you, sir."

"Be gone with you," he barked. "You cannot possibly be of any help to me."

The old woman's eyes were glued on his. "But I can, sir. For the great spirits have sent me to you. For you have been cursed by an enemy. For only a mere five dollars, I can remove the spell."

Holton was a God-fearing Episcopalian and a practical man with no patience for this foolishness. "Get out of here, you thieving gypsy!" he roared.

Did the image of the gypsy woman's face invade Holton's dreams? *From www.pixabay.com.*

The old woman held her ground. The more he shouted insults at her, the more intently she glared at him. "You are doomed if you do not allow me to remove the curse. The cost is small; one you can well afford."

Holton lost patience with the old woman. "Get out of here before I call the dog out on you," he bellowed. He shoved the old woman away from the door. She toppled off the doorstep and into the wet shrubbery. As he turned to close the door, the old woman appeared from the shrubs. "You scorn the gypsy. You are now duly cursed, Oliver Holton!" She raised her arms skyward before sweeping them toward him. Her long fingers pointed at his face. "The malevolence of the *Canis lupus*, the immortal one, will shadow you always and will, within two harvest moons, rip apart and devour what all is yours." Holton slammed the door and shook his head. When he returned to dinner, he reminded his wife to be certain to lock the doors the following day, as there were gypsies in the area. He thought no more of the encounter.

Oliver Holton was a man with an entrepreneurial spirit, as well as an interest in exotic wildlife. It is likely this interest in unusual and peculiar animals prompted him to purchase a 214-acre farm in Middletown, New Jersey, in the early 1920s. It was located in the area that is now bordered by Twinbrook and Woodland Drives, on the southbound side of Route 35. The homestead, which was then known as Twinbrook Farm, eventually became his pride and joy, Twinbrook Zoological Park. But Oliver Holton's life was far from idyllic.

Shortly after his encounter with the gypsy, Holton began a venture in poultry distribution. He bought large quantities of ducks, geese and chickens and resold them to local farmers. But the venture was short-lived, as a disease killed the bulk of his stock within a few months.

Holton quickly revised his business plan; he decided to open his dream attraction, a zoological park, where exotic beasts from around the world would be displayed. He knew many of these beasts were extremely popular at a larger zoo in New York City. His Twinbrook Zoo would enable people from all over the East Coast to observe such creatures without going into New York. He was certain it would be a success.

In early 1925, he began building the zoo by purchasing a collection of wild game birds. Within a few days, a pack of what was described as wild dogs broke through the enclosure and decimated the collection. Although a search was made, the culprits were not caught. Not to be defeated, Holton built a sturdy compound to house his animal collection. He reinforced the structures and quickly began purchasing a wide variety of wild creatures. He bought specimens from other zoos and circuses, and he made private purchases from well-known wild animal hunters and collectors. Despite three additional run-ins with the wild dogs in the area, the zoo opened on May 1, 1926. The public was enthralled, and the zoo became an instant success. Normally, there were long lines of visitors waiting to see his collection of elephants, lions, tigers, monkeys, large Amazonian snakes, wolves, bears, flamingoes and other exotic beasts.

Within days, more problems arose when several monkeys repeatedly escaped their cages, causing chaos and destruction in the neighboring areas. Each time they escaped, Holton sent out search parties to track down the miscreants, and he quickly paid for the cost of their destruction. More than a few neighbors began to complain among themselves about the security of the zoo.

Then, in July, an extremely rare spotted leopard arrived from India. Unfortunately, the animal arrived earlier than expected, and its permanent enclosure was not complete. Within an hour of arrival, the leopard had managed to escape from his travel crate. To make matters worse, the leopard's absence wasn't noticed immediately. By the time the alarm was sounded, the huge cat was nowhere to be found. Holton was beside himself with worry. Not only had the cat been extremely expensive, but it was undoubtedly dangerous to humans and other animals. He hired a search party, which scoured the area with no success.

For a time, the cat was only seen by a five-year-old girl, Margaret Ellison, from nearby Nutswamp. The girl saw the leopard and reported to her father that she had seen a big, ugly dog covered with spots in the orchard. Despite an intense search, nothing was found. Initially, Holton did not report the missing leopard to the authorities, as he believed his hired posse would do a better job of tracking down and capturing the animal. It was not until several additional sightings of the animal were reported to the police that Holton confirmed the cat was missing.

The local authorities never made attempts to capture the creature. They forwarded all sightings to Holton, who checked out every report. With the missing leopard causing such a fuss, Holton offered a $100 reward for the animal's return—dead or alive (that is about $1,500 in today's money). Hunters from around the state joined the search in hopes of capturing the reward. The missing leopard became front-page news. The *Daily Register* printed reports of sightings in nearly every edition. Red Bank storekeepers used images of the leopard as advertising, and it is said that a road crew was once fired because they wouldn't stop talking about the missing leopard and some migrant blackberry pickers refused to go back to the field for a time.

Holton tried everything he could to capture the beast. In addition to his long-standing search parties, he set live bait traps in the woods and obtained special scents from the department of interior to bait the creature, but they were all unsuccessful. Despite his preoccupation with the missing leopard, Holton continued adding more animals to his zoological park.

After a few weeks without further sightings, interest in the cat died down. Rumors persisted that Holton had invented the missing cat as a publicity stunt for his zoo.

Nearly four months after the disappearance, Willard Irons, a young farmer from Island Heights, began to notice his ducks were disappearing from his pond. He never considered a leopard was the culprit, as Middletown was over forty miles away from his farm. One day, he heard his mother screaming from the pond. He snatched his shotgun and ran toward her screams. The spotted leopard had caught its paw in a beaver trap and was fiercely attempting to free itself. Irons dispatched the leopard by firing both barrels of his shotgun into its head. He showed the dead cat to a neighbor, who reminded him of the missing leopard in Middletown. Irons telephoned Mr. Holton, put the animal in the back of his car and drove it to Middletown. Anxious to settle the capture of the animal, Holton arranged for Dan Dorn, a Red Bank photographer, to photograph the return and display of the leopard. The matter died down, and Holton's string of bad luck appeared to be over.

The zoo closed for the winter, and most of the animals were housed at the Steel Pier in Atlantic City. They were returned to Middletown in the early spring of 1927. Holton was anxious for spring and was hopeful for a successful, uneventful summer—but that would not be the case. The season at the zoo began without incident. The crowds were large, and the intake was impressive. In early July, Mrs. Holton and the couple's eldest son set out to visit relatives in Pennsylvania for a few days. Mr. Holton; his two-year-old son, Teddy; and the family cook, Mrs. Mazza, remained at the zoo. On July 20, Mr. Holton was working on repairs at an enclosure at the zoo while his son Teddy was playing with the cook's five-year-old son, Henry, in the family's yard. Their family dog, a trusted German Shepard named Duke, watched as the children darted around the lawn. Duke was so well trained that he let himself in and out of the house by opening the back screen door with his nose. Suddenly, Henry ran into the kitchen with blood running down his ear. "A big dog is biting Teddy!" he screeched. Mrs. Mazza dashed toward the door and shouted at Henry to stay inside the house. She grabbed the first thing she saw, a broom, and ran out to confront the dog.

She gasped in terror. A large gray wolf was tossing little Teddy around as if he were a doll. She began beating the head of the wolf. Finally, the beast let loose of the child for a moment. In that instant, Mrs. Mazza snatched up the little boy. As she ran toward the house, she saw in horror that her own son had disobeyed and was standing in the yard watching the event. She held the bleeding toddler in one arm, grasped her son in the other and raced back into the kitchen. The boy was bitten but seemed to not be critically injured. She laid the child on the couch and ran to get a gun. She found the shotgun, but there was no ammunition to be found. Then she heard her son scream, "No, Duke! Don't open the door!"

Teddy's screams brought Mrs. Mazza back into the room. The wolf was in the house and was attacking the hysterical child. She raised the gun to strike the wolf, but it snatched the bleeding toddler and ran outside. Mazza chased the animal with the empty gun. She bashed the head of the wolf with all her strength. Stunned, the wolf finally dropped the motionless child and loped to the side yard before it disappeared.

A worker, on hearing the noise, alerted the crew at the zoo. Mr. Holton arrived and sent men to dispatch the wolf. The children were taken to Woodley Hospital in Red Bank. Henry survived with a few bites and scratches. Teddy Holton, Oliver Holton's son, was not so lucky. The second attack of the wolf had punctured Teddy's lung in several places. Despite massive efforts to save the child, he died the following day. The gray lobo wolf, *Canis lupus*, which keepers believed to be tame, had escaped his enclosure and killed the child. Staffers who were later interviewed claimed the wolf was so tame they could pet him and that Duke, the family dog, could enter the wolf's enclosure without incident.

After the funeral, Mrs. Holton and their other son returned to Pennsylvania. The zoo reopened for a few weeks, but Mr. Holton had lost his obsession with his zoological park. By October 16, 1927, the zoo was officially closed. News of the tragedy had spread across the area. The community became extremely vocal about their concerns for their safety.

Canis lupus, the grey wolf they all believed to be so tame, destroyed Holton's dream. *From www.commons. wikimedia.net.*

Holton was called to a town council meeting where he was so devastated that he made no defense and informed the town council that he was selling off the animals immediately.

Holton sold some of the animals to zoos and circuses. Large quantities of snake and poultry meat were purchased by a meat wholesaler. Soon afterward, Oliver Holton put the farm, the zoo and all the property on the market. The property was finally sold in May 1928. As if Holton needed any more bad luck, his wife soon divorced him, taking their other son with her.

Oliver William Holton had combined his interest in exotic animals with his entrepreneurial skills in an effort to provide for his family. Despite his best efforts, he suffered mishap after mishap in his business ventures. Finally, the devastating loss of his son and the resulting loss of his wife and family annihilated his lifelong dreams. They had literally been devoured by the jaws of *Canis lupus*, just as the gypsy predicted.

The last anyone heard of Oliver Holton was that he left the United States for Central America. We can only speculate his final destination. Was he in search of new exotic animals, or was he in search of something else? Perhaps he was seeking the old gypsy or anyone or anything that could remove the curse of the *Canis lupus*.

5
TALE OF TWO CEMETERIES

This is the tale of two cemeteries. There is nothing particularly unique about either one. Neither is home to countless screen stars, like Forrest Lawn in Hollywood. And neither is as historic as Highgate in London, where countless leaders of industry, politics and the arts rest in peace. Fairview and Bay View Cemeteries are prominent local burial grounds in Middletown Township. Admittedly, there are numerous other cemeteries and church graveyards in the region, but these two hold unique tales of supernatural happenings.

One of the largest private non-sectarian burial spots in the area is Fairview Cemetery. It is located in Middletown along Highway 35 and Chapel Hill Road in the old area that was once referred to as Hedden's Corner. It is a sprawling, well-manicured parklike setting, with a series of winding paved lanes that intertwine throughout the immaculately landscaped property.

Established in 1851, just before the Civil War, Fairview is home to more than twenty-one thousand graves. Between spring and autumn, Fairview bursts with fresh colorful plantings, established flower beds, beautiful trees and ornamental vegetation. It has a charming atmosphere. Yet, curious accounts have surfaced about this cemetery, revealing that, sometimes, things aren't exactly what they seem. Fairview has its share of strange, even extraordinary, events. While some burial grounds tend to have one specific apparition or unexplained event, Fairview has several. Firsthand accounts reveal some startling details.

Fairview Cemetery has graves from the earliest days of New Jersey. *Photograph by author.*

THE LADY IN WHITE

One of the most widely reported apparitions at Fairview is known as the Victorian Lady or the Lady in White. The ghostly caller has been seen on many occasions by both staff and visitors for many years. Most agree on her description. The figure is a woman of slight build with an elaborate hairstyle. A rope of pearls, white feathers and sprays of lily of the valley encompasses her hair, which falls gently down her back. Both her features and clothing are stark white. She wears an elegant Victorian gown with long lace sleeves and a high neckline. Her waist is cinched tightly, held in place by a single red rose. Her hoop skirt balloons away from her waist in great folds of sheer white fabric. She moves purposefully across the plots as if in search of something, with movements so graceful that she appears to be floating just inches above the ground.

Those who have seen her from afar claim that she appears to be almost transparent and that she seems oblivious to anyone near. Others who have come upon her suddenly assert that they usually see her out of the corners of their eyes. Some claim to have observed her for several minutes in this manner, but they said when they approached or attempted to look at her squarely in the face, she evaporated before their eyes. Those familiar with the cemetery are accustomed to her frequent visits and make no attempt to interfere with her meanderings. Whenever visitors ask staff about the strange woman in old-fashioned clothes, they reply, "Oh, that is the Lady in White."

Ghost Rain

Fairview has another highly irregular phenomenon, which has yet to be explained—the ghost rain. This manifestation has been seen dozens of times over the years, particularly by the crews performing their landscaping duties. The ghost rain occurs only in the very oldest part of the cemetery, over by a stand of beautiful old birch trees. It nearly always occurs on a fairly overcast day but not one that threatens any kind of precipitation. As the team of workers approach the old section with their power tools and mowers, they see ahead of them that it is raining. It is not just a light drizzle; it appears to be a downpour, drenching the grounds of the old section. Anxious not to destroy their equipment, they quickly pack up and head for shelter. If anyone rushes to the deluge, they find the soil bone dry. This phenomenon is repeated multiple times during the summer months.

The Paupers' Field Ghost

Until recently, the State of New Jersey required that all licensed cemeteries set aside a portion of their property to provide burial for the indigent and homeless. In return, the government provided a small stipend for the preparation and closing of the graves. These sad burials were seldom attended by either family or friends. Most of these graves are unmarked and are devoid of floral arrangements or family remembrances. The local funeral directors, under the same regulations as the cemeteries, provided minimal service for these burials. The unfortunate were buried there, without vaults, sometimes five deep, in thin particleboard coffins.

Few visitors make their way to that section of the cemetery, and if they do, they seldom linger. First, there was an unpleasant aroma in the area, and then, there was the phantom. Both visitors and staff have witnessed a gangly old man dressed in old rags and a dirty misshaped fedora standing in Paupers' Field. The presence is known as the Paupers' Field Ghost. Sometimes, he simply stands in the center of the field and beckons others to come his way. Other times, he is seen pacing back and forth amid the unmarked graves. His ragged clothes and unkempt appearance never change. Crews have reported that the phantom is seen most frequently when they are mowing in the field. He moves back and forth across the plot, seemingly supervising the mowing operation. Perhaps he is ensuring these graves are properly attended. Others insist that when someone does wander into the area, the ragged man suddenly appears, as if providing security for the lonely outpost.

The Children's Graveyard

In a secluded section of the cemetery, along Chapel Hill Road, there is an old children's cemetery. It is a small collection of children's graves that are partially obscured by a small grove of dogwood trees and small shrubbery. This area has been part of the cemetery since its earliest days, with markers going back into the early 1800s. They are all the graves of small children. They belong to no particular family; rather, they are just a gathering of little ones resting together beneath the canopy of dogwoods overhead.

Many visitors who come upon the scene stop to stare at the collection of stones. Visitors often return to these plots, leaving toys, dolls and stuffed animals. These forlorn little graves hold a special place in the hearts of the crew, who check on these plots daily, often adding small plantings of flowers. Frequently, they find that toys that were left on the graves have moved during the night to a different plot. Sometimes, one or two disappear, or a new one is added overnight. In one incident, a bright-red rubber ball was left on a young boy's grave. Over a few days, the staff noticed that the ball had been moved to another grave. For some time, the ball moved daily from one grave to another. After a while, the weathered and faded ball was removed from the grave and carried to the other end of the cemetery, where the trash was collected. The next morning, when the crew checked on the children's cemetery, the ball was back on the boy's grave.

COOKING A GRAVE

Most of us don't give much thought as to how difficult it must be to dig a grave in the winter. In our area, from November to April, the ground can be frozen up to two feet deep. During the most frigid parts of the winter, even a jackhammer can have trouble breaking through the frozen earth. But just like life, death goes on all throughout winter. So, what does the cemetery do? Well, they cook the grave.

Technology has made this an easier task than it was in the past, but it is by no means a simple or inexpensive process. Cemeteries use a piece of equipment known as a grave burner to heat the earth enough so that a grave can be prepared. The burner is a rectangular metal appliance that is placed on the exact site of the desired grave. The device resembles a domed rectangular lid. Beneath the lid are a series of butane burners. Huge tanks of butane are connected to the burners, and the apparatus operates for hours, literally roasting the earth so that it is softened. Then, it must keep the soil soft until the grave can be dug. Since the apparatus must run for hours, the butane tanks supplying the energy must be replenished so that the burners do not go out. If they do, the earth will refreeze before the grave can be dug.

The length of the process usually means that the burner is put into operation the day before the grave is scheduled to be opened. It is kept in operation overnight so that the soil is soft in the morning. During the night, usually around 3:00 a.m., fresh butane tanks must replace the empty ones at the grave site. This unpleasant and frigid task is done by a team of two men, who lug a new canister of butane to the grave site, replace the old one and reconnect the burners. It isn't a job anyone ever volunteers for.

On such a night, in the middle of February in the 1970s, two workers left their warm beds and headed to the cemetery to switch the butane tanks. They came prepared, wearing heavy coats, wool hats and thick work gloves. They met at the supply shed and grabbed some lanterns, a couple of flashlights and a huge butane tank. The tank was heavy, so they loaded it on a small hand cart, which they wheeled along the roadway until it ended. Then, they moved along a cobblestone path until they reached the site near the grave burner. Then, they hoisted the heavy canister over the frozen turf to the grave site. They knew at once that the burner was doing its job, as the aroma of roasted chestnuts filled the air; this told them the earth beneath was warm and workable. By then, their hands and fingers were numb from the cold, but they swiftly disconnected the old tank and reconnected the nozzle to the new butane cylinder. One man checked to see that the burner was lit, while the other tossed the empty tank into their cart.

Just then, out of the icy darkness, they heard a curious sound. It wasn't an animal, and there was no traffic on the highway that time of night. It took them a moment before they recognized the sound. It was the dull thudding sound of a horse walking across frozen earth. They peered into the darkness of the cemetery but could see nothing. The *thud-d-thud* was coming closer, and with it came the additional creak of an old wagon wheel. Someone was nearby with a horse and wagon. Although they scoured the area with their flashlights, they saw nothing. They couldn't imagine who would be out on a night like that. Yet, the thudding grew louder and louder.

Suddenly, the clatter of horses on an earthen path became the distinctive *clop-clap* sound of a horse and wagon moving across cobblestones. They both turned to face the commotion in the darkness. One of the men snatched a small flashlight, and without speaking, they raced toward the sound. They darted between the grave markers until they reached the cobblestone path, but they saw nothing. There was only the icy black air and silence—perfect silence. Although they shone their flashlights in every direction, the cemetery lay silent and still, blanketed in the cold and dark. The two quickly gathered their equipment and hurried back to the supply shed in total silence. When they did speak, they agreed to wait until morning to tell Old Herb, the caretaker, what they had heard. The next morning, when they described the event to the caretaker, he merely grinned and with a chuckle said, "So, what else is new, boys?"

Speaking of the Old Caretaker

Old Herb, as they called him, had worked at the cemetery as long as anyone could remember. No one knew how old he was, although he looked to be nearly one hundred; no one who worked there was about to ask. Everyone liked Old Herb. He made certain that everyone did their work and did it correctly. Yet, he was full of stories and enjoyed a good laugh and cold beer at the end of a shift. He lived in a small cottage at the very center of the sprawling cemetery. It was a cozy, secluded spot with room for a small garden and bird feeders. Best of all, according to Herb, was that his neighbors never threw loud parties or asked to borrow anything.

The frequent ghostly encounters at Fairview are witnessed by both staff and guests. *Photograph by author.*

When it suited him, Old Herb shared tales of the cemetery. He described hearing the same sounds the grave burner crew had witnessed. He attributed that to the fact that the older hearses, before the era of automobiles, were indeed horse wagons. "So, in such cases," he said, "it is best to just let it be." He said he heard laughter and, sometimes, crying throughout the grounds late at night. Although he investigated, expecting to find intruders, the result was always the same—there was no one there. As he grew older, Old Herb continued his peaceful coexistence with his neighbors. They didn't come visiting him at night, and likewise, he no longer entered the cemetery after dark. When asked why, he responded, "When you live and work in a cemetery, you see things."

BAYVIEW CEMETERY

Bayview Cemetery is a small, secluded burial ground located off of Hosford Avenue in Middletown. The isolated cemetery houses three thousand graves, many of which date from the early days of Monmouth County. The cemetery is set in a quiet woodland area, well away from the hustle and bustle of modern-day life. The gated property is open for several hours each day for visitation, but it closes before dusk.

For some years, paranormal enthusiasts have called this burial ground Greenlight Cemetery due to the curious happenings there. The burial grounds garnered the nickname after numerous reports were made of a bright-green light glimmering within the cemetery on certain nights, creating curious paranormal anomalies. There were often disagreements about the actual origins of the strange light. Certain reports indicate that the light emanated from the cemetery itself. Others claim that the light seemed to originate at the tree line and shone directly into the cemetery.

Accounts of these events have been published widely in local newspapers, magazines and books. One *Weird N.J.* account claims that the greenish light comes from an old caretaker who once lived near the site. It's said that he holds a greenish lantern out so the spirits of the dead can find their way back to their graves.

Another insists that if you follow the green light, seeking its source, you will be consumed by the surrounding green forest. Still others claim that when the light is visible, other apparitions and manifestations can also be seen and heard. Most accounts agree that the phenomenon of the green glow is sporadic and that one must be patient in order to see the spectral event.

According to some, the greenish glow is sometimes accompanied by the apparition of a group of three small children playing among the grave markers. The three are all girls, dressed in old-fashioned clothes. They appear to be singing some sort of song or rhyme that is barely audible. One can definitely hear giggles and joyful squeals as the specters run about in the greenish glow. Reports insist that if the children are approached or beckoned, they suddenly disappear.

Yet another account claims that a woman in old-fashioned widow's weeds paces methodically through the grounds. It's said she wears a long black dress and a black hat with a long veil. She appears to be reading the names and inscriptions on each and every grave marker. She approaches each grave gingerly and bends over to peer at the writing carved into the stone. She shakes her head, stands erect and begins wringing her hands. Then, she moves to the next marker and repeats the procedure. It is said that the apparition appears only when the green light is illuminating the cemetery. She will remain there for long periods of time unless she is interrupted. Should anyone approach her or call out, she vanishes.

Another account associated with the green light comes from several sources. Near the front gate, but off to one side, there are a few small, weathered headstones. The markers are very old, and the graves no longer receive visitors. Some have claimed that when they visit the cemetery and pass by the group of small stones, a small whisper is heard saying, "Please don't leave me." The lonely, ethereal voice has beckoned callers for many years, seeking a few more moments of human contact. Interestingly, one gatekeeper also reports that he's heard soft crying when locking the gates for the night. It seems that some of the spirits at Bayview have grown lonely.

It is unknown what has happened to the green light at Bayview. Does it still appear? And what has happened to those auxiliary manifestations? Do the children still play among the weathered stones? Does the widow still search the old grave markers? And do the deserted spirits still cry out in their loneliness?

6

AN APPARITION IN THE ICE

Another anecdote from the long and colorful history of the Navesink River unites a period of great excitement with a local tragedy, resulting in an unexplained series of events. Around the time of the Civil War, as the nation struggled to stay united, a new and exciting winter sport was born on the Navesink. Although the ice sled had been used to transport supplies for some time by both Europeans and the early American colonists, its use as a recreational vehicle first gained popularity on the area's rivers.

George Allaire and Nathan Cook are credited with building and sailing the first Navesink iceboat in 1865. It immediately became the talk of the entire waterfront. It wasn't long before others joined in the frosty adventure. Soon, a multitude of homemade boats of every conceivable style and form were sharing the frozen river. Everyone seemed to have their own favorites, but eventually, the three-runner masted boat became the most popular model. Almost immediately, iceboats were being commercially produced. It wasn't long before the Navesink gained national attention. People came from great distances to participate and observe the iceboaters on the frozen river. By 1880, the North Shrewsbury Iceboat and Yacht Club was formed. Soon, weather permitting, the river was alive with the sound of flapping sails and the scratch of runners gliding on the icy river. There were races between the two bridges, winter ice carnivals and regattas. Even Thomas A. Edison brought his newly invented movie camera to Red Bank three times between 1900 and 1903 to film the iceboats in action.

Iceboating remains extremely popular, hampered only by a recent trend of warmer winters. The significance of iceboating cannot be overstated. Organizers from the club have been instrumental in developing and maintaining safety on the river. During the iceboating season, there are hourly depth checks, temperature monitoring, clearly identified course paths, hazard warning signs and even boat inspections. Every possible effort is made to ensure safety on the ice. There were, of course, numerous minor mishaps and crashes over the years, but nothing serious happened until February 12, 1906.

That Sunday morning was bitterly cold. The ice had been frozen solid for several days. When the wind picked up that morning, iceboating enthusiasts headed for the river. The Navesink appeared to be solid off the Fair Haven dock when Charles and Benjamin Hendrickson hurried to join the dozens of other iceboaters taking advantage of the smooth, glistening ice. Bundled in long johns and two layers of clothes, as well as heavy coats, gloves and scarves, the two brothers set out for a day of fun.

With the younger brother, Benjamin, as the pilot, they sped up and down the river, with the icy wind smacking their faces. They were both laughing so hard that they failed to keep a sharp lookout for thin ice. Without warning, their boat crashed through a soft spot in the ice, plunging the two brothers headfirst into the icy water. Benjamin escaped by clinging to the windward runner, but his brother was not so lucky. Charles was plunged deep into the icy Navesink. Despite his brother's valiant efforts to save him, he was trapped beneath the ice and drowned.

It was an emotional scene, as rescuers used oyster tongs to drag the area of the river where the boy fell in. After about an hour, his lifeless body was returned to the surface. Despite attempts of resuscitation, Charles was pronounced dead at the scene. For some years after the event, numerous witnesses alleged to have seen an apparition of the drowned teen frozen in the ice. The grotesque apparition is seen only in early February, when the temperatures are the most frigid. Witnesses maintain that the face of the drowned victim is smeared against the ice, contorted in pain and fear. Some claim to hear garbled cries for help from beneath the ice. Others insist that they were so terrified, they fled the river, leaving their iceboats behind.

By 1940, there were many versions of the story, few of which reflected the true details from the newspaper accounts of the event. Although fathers and grandfathers retold the story repeatedly to warn their sons of the dangers of thin ice, it never dampened the youngsters' enthusiasm for iceboating.

Frank and Burt were no exception. The eleven-year-old twins had lived their entire lives along the Navesink. They swam there before they could walk and sailed homemade rafts they had built from scraps of lumber, and during the summer, they dug for clams with their father for their evening supper. The boys loved fishing, swimming, sailing and especially iceboating. They loved to do anything on the river and any activity that did not involve long division or Reverend Forman's long sermons.

Frank and Burt had heard all the different accounts of the accident but didn't believe a single word of those who claimed to have seen the apparition. Earlier, they had scoffed at their classmate Billy, who claimed his uncle had seen the apparition of the drowned boy. It had been a mild winter, so when the deep chill first appeared in early February, the boys became eager for their first iceboating trip of the winter. They hurried to the iceboat shed every afternoon, right after school, and began preparing their iceboat for its first run of the winter. There was wood to polish and blades to sharpen. The twins were finishing their work on the blades when Frankie tossed his rag into the air, exclaiming, "I've got it!" Although Burt was the older twin by at least ten full minutes, it was Frankie who first came up with the idea.

"You got what?" Burt looked up at his brother and frowned. He knew that look on Frankie's face. That look usually meant trouble.

"I know how to get even with Billy." Frankie crowed, "I'll fix him. He even had the girls crowding around him when he bragged about his uncle seeing the face in the ice." Burt's face took on a worried look, but before he could speak, Frankie went on. "We'll tell everyone that we saw the face ourselves. That's better than some dumb uncle seeing it."

"I d—d—d—don't know, Frankie," Burt countered.

"Stop stuttering," Frank commanded. "It's a great idea. Listen, you don't have to talk at all. All you do is stand there. Nod your head while I am talking and agree to everything I say. Got it?"

The frown on Burt's face softened. "Are you sure it will work? We could get into a lot of trouble."

"Of course it will work. I got it all figured out. I'll lay it on thick, too. We'll scare the girls good." Frankie gleefully grabbed his cloth and continued polishing the iceboat.

The next morning, Frankie was already in homeroom when the bell rang. As his classmates filed in, the room filled with chatter, laughter and the sound of bodies plopping into chairs. "Hey, Billy, that face your uncle saw on the ice is a fake," Frankie shouted above the din. "Burt and I saw the real one. It was nothing like that sorry one you claim your uncle saw." Burt swallowed hard and took a deep breath; Frankie was at it again.

Billy taunted, "Oh, yeah? I don't believe it. So, what did it look like?"

Although he was speaking to Billy, thirty sets of eyes were locked onto Frankie. As he began to speak, the class eased from their chairs and moved closer and closer until they formed a circle around the two boys. Frankie began to speak hurriedly. "Well, two nights ago, it was nearly dark. Burt and I went to check to see if the ice was ready for the weekend."

"Your dad didn't let you do that," Billy challenged. "Only grownups do ice checks."

"Do you want to hear about the monster or not?" Frankie asked.

Murmurs of "Monster! What monster?" bounced around the room.

"We were out on the ice looking for soft spots, over by the old pilings on the north side, and that is when we heard the moan," Frankie said.

"You said you saw it," Billy interrupted.

"We did, but we heard it, too. It moaned like someone was stabbing it with a sword, and then it screamed bloody murder! It was coming from under the ice. I kid you not. Right, Burt?" Burt managed a small nod of his head.

"It was horrible, like something suffering and angry at the same time. But then, we looked at the ice and saw it." The group gasped, and two of the girls hugged one another.

Someone urged, "Go on!"

"There it was, a face—well, kind of a face." Frankie paused to let it sink in. "It kind of looked human, but it wasn't really human. It was like a dead goat or maybe a bear with hatchet marks all over it and more like a dead body all rotten and jelly-like." Moans filled the air. "The face of whatever it is was smeared up against the ice, and it was looking right at us. There were purple scars with maggots and blood oozing from its squashed nose. The eyes were out of their sockets and bulged as if coming right out of the ice. There was green glowing slime everywhere, and the eyeballs followed us when we moved."

Frankie knew he had their undivided attention now. He began describing how a moaning screechy voice came from the grotesque creature, pleading, "Children, children, I want children. Bring me children." The boys looked at one another with wide eyes, several girls screamed and Molly and Patty ran from the room crying. "It was the most grotesque and disgusting thing you ever saw. And smell, did I tell you it smelled like an old outhouse?" Frankie added. "And you know what the worst part was? That—"

At that moment, Miss Price entered the classroom with Molly and Patty in tow. Her normal smile was upside down, "Franklin, what is going on?"

Frankie froze; he could feel her eyes fixed on him. "What did you do to make these girls cry?" she demanded.

Frankie gave her his most innocent look. "Oh, it was nothing, Miss Price. I was just telling everyone that Burt and me saw the apparition on the river."

"That is Burt and I, young man. Watch your grammar." She turned to the class. "Everyone, to your seats. Now!" Instantly, the circle melted as everyone hurried to their seats. Burt crept into his chair trying to make himself invisible. "Frankie, I don't want to hear another word about that superstition. Do you understand?"

"Yes, Miss Price. I was only—"

"Not another word!" Miss Price turned to face Burt, who was huddled so tightly in his seat that he had nearly turned himself into a ball. "Were you in on this as well, Burt?"

Burt tried to answer, but he could only stutter, "I—I—I—I—"

"Never mind, Burt," her voice softened. "Boys, I will be speaking with your father about this, and when I do, I will mention those dreadful spelling tests last week." It was the longest afternoon either boy could remember having, but the night was even longer. When Frankie and Burton arrived home after school, their father was waiting for them at the front door. "Hey, Dad, you're home early," Frankie exclaimed.

"Don't you 'Hey Dad' me, mister! Both of you get in this house this instant!" The boys looked at one another; they knew they were in trouble. They slowly followed their father to the living room. As expected, their father scolded them both for disrupting class, for making the girls cry and especially for making up stories. Not only was he deeply disappointed in his two sons who bore his name, but the entire family was embarrassed by their actions. He seemed to go on and on even longer than Reverend Forman's sermons.

Finally, their father told them the consequence for their disgraceful conduct in school. Their planned iceboating day on the river that Sunday was cancelled. When Frankie started to protest, his father warned, "I am not done yet, young man." In addition, the boys would be dropped off at church on Sunday morning. They would attend both the long worship service and Sunday school and then would help Mrs. Murphy with the refreshments for the coffee hour and clean up the church hall afterward. They would be there for at least four hours.

"We were just—" Frankie tried to speak.

"Stop. No excuses," their father said. "Since I can't iceboat alone, I will take your mother for a nice Sunday brunch down along the shore. We will be back in the afternoon. When you finish helping Mrs. Murphy cleaning up the church hall, you will walk her home and take her dog for its afternoon walk and do any chores she may have for you."

"Dad! That reverend talks for hours and hours, and Mrs. Murphy—that dog of hers stinks."

"Enough!" their dad shouted and walked away.

The twins looked at one another. Could there have been any worse punishment? The next day was Saturday, and that meant it was chore day for everyone. The boys were grim as they started their tasks, as they had nothing to look forward to for the entire weekend. Their father had barely spoken to them except to remind them that they needed to have all their chores done by supper time. As the boys were gathering logs for the fireplace, Frankie muttered to himself about the unfairness of the punishment. He grabbed a fireplace log and tossed it to Burt, who caught it and stacked it in the log shuttle. "It isn't fair! This is the first good ice of the winter, and we are going to miss it, all just because some dumb girl was blubbering all over the teacher."

"I don't know," Burt sighed. "You did make it sound scary. There must be some way we could convince Dad to take us iceboating tomorrow. Maybe if we promised never ever again to make the girls cry?"

"Nah," Frankie said. "That won't work." Frankie was quiet for a few minutes, and then he shrieked, "I got it! I know how we can go iceboating!"

"Frankie, no way. We can't go iceboating. Dad said so."

"Here's the plan, Burt. Just listen." As they worked, Frankie laid out his plan. First, when they went back inside Frankie would sneak upstairs while Burt was loading the log shuttle. He would then gather all their iceboating clothes, jackets, pants, boots, gloves and hats and tie them into one of their bedsheets. Burt's eyes were wide, and he kept shaking his head back and forth. Frankie ignored him and went on to explain that they would work hard and finish all the chores. After supper, they would volunteer to do the dishes and clean up the kitchen for their mom. Then, while they were doing that, Frankie would sneak up and toss the bundle out the window, onto the lawn. "Then, when we take out the garbage, we'll grab the clothes and stash them in the iceboat until tomorrow." Burt let out a soft moan. "The rest will be easy," Frankie continued. "We'll dress up and go to church, just like Dad said. As soon as Dad leaves, we'll double back home and go iceboating. Mom and Dad won't be home until late afternoon."

"Oh, I don't know, Frankie. It sounds complicated," Burt mumbled.

"It's perfect. We'll have time for a couple great rides on the ice and still have time to come back and change back into our Sunday clothes," Frankie smiled at his plan. "Never mind, all you need to do is back me up, no matter what happens."

Everything went according to plan. When Frankie and Burt offered to clean up for their mom, she gave them a smile. "My sweet boys, I'm so proud of you," she cooed, giving each a kiss on the forehead before hurrying to join their father in the living room. As quickly as they could, they did all the dishes and cleaned the kitchen. While Burt scrubbed the last of the pots, Frankie crept upstairs and tossed the bag of iceboat clothes out the bedroom window, onto the lawn. With that done, they hurried to take out the garbage. They snatched the bag of clothes from the lawn and quickly stashed the bundle in the iceboat.

It was even colder the next morning, when Burt and Frankie were dropped off in front of the church just before 9:00 a.m. They were dressed in their Sunday best; their mom kept saying how handsome they looked, and their dad gave them money for the collection. He reminded them that they must stay for both services and help Mrs. Murphy with refreshments for coffee hour. Finally, he added, "And one more thing, boys—no snowball fights in your good clothes. And only one piece of cake, even if they offer you more. Got it?"

"Yes sir," they answered in unison.

The boys waved goodbye to their parents and walked slowly up the steps of the church. They stepped aside to let an older couple enter. Just as the door closed, Frankie grabbed Burt by the sleeve and yanked him along as he darted into the evergreen shrubbery that surrounded the building. They sat among the thick greens until they were sure no one had seen them. They moved quickly through the prickly underbrush until they reached the corner near the rear parking lot. They darted across the lawn and onto the street. From there, they doubled back, being careful to avoid neighbors. When they got to their house, they ran straight to the iceboat shed. The temperature was in the twenties, and the boys shivered as they changed into their winter clothes. "Frankie, you didn't bring our long johns; we're gonna freeze," Burt grumbled.

Frankie was dressed by then and opened the doors to the ice shed as Burt finished getting his boots tied. He rushed to the water's edge and ran out onto the ice, sliding until he fell over. He smacked the ice hard with his fist. "See?" he yelled to Burt. "Solid as a rock. Come on, we'll just do a couple rides, put the boat back and be back home before Mom and Dad."

"Are you sure we should do this alone?" Burt asked.

"You're such an old Nelly. What are you talking about? Look at the river. There are a dozen boats out there already. Come on! Time's a wasting."

They shoved and tugged and finally, with one big yank, slid the iceboat out onto the frozen Navesink. Frankie pushed the boat farther out onto the river for a better position, while Burt carefully adjusted the sail so it could catch the wind, just as his father had taught him. The boat began to glide across the ice. Frankie jumped into the pilot seat. "Come on, Burt. Get onboard," he called. Burt caught hold of the mast and swung himself into position. The instant he adjusted the sail, the little boat seemed to take flight. The boys were hurtling down the river faster than they had ever done before. Suddenly, loud curses came at them from another boat. "Watch where you are going! You're going to kill somebody!" The boys had been laughing so hard that they had paid little attention to the other iceboats on the river.

"You got to steer!" Burt shouted.

"I'm trying, I'm trying!" Frankie screeched. Just then, he looked ahead and saw a much larger boat bearing down on them. It was directly ahead and coming in fast. Frankie yanked on the tiller as hard as he could, and the little boat went sideways, toward the far bank. At that moment, a cross wind swept the boat around in a circle, and the boys flew from the boat and landed on the hard ice. Frankie sat up first and searched for his brother. Burt lay on the ice near the overturned boat. Frankie held his breath as he approached; just then, Burt sat up, rubbing a scrape on his chin. Frankie whooped, "That was some ride, wasn't it?"

"Let's hope we didn't wreck the boat," Burt muttered as he began to inspect the mast. After deciding they needed to get the craft upright, Frankie moved around to the other side of the boat to help lift.

"Okay," Frank ordered, "when I say 'three,' you lift your side." Frankie had just counted to two when Burt saw it. "Fr—Fra—Fran—Frank—k—k—eee—Frankkkie!" Burt shrieked and dropped the boat onto the ice.

"Come on, you donkey. I can't lift this by myself, I—" Frankie never finished.

"You better come—come over here—" Burt screeched.

Frankie muttered to himself as he let the boat gently back onto the ice. He looked at his brother, who was shaking like a leaf and pointing to a spot on the ice. "Don't tell me we broke it," Frankie said as he hurried to where Burt was standing. Then, he saw it too. There it was—the face. Not just any face—that face. It was the very same face Frankie had described in school. Then, from the ice, just a few feet from the boat, came a moaning sound; it sounded like someone being stabbed by a sword, and then it screamed. It screamed and screamed—it screamed bloody murder.

The boys were frozen in place. The creature looked like it was suffering terribly and, at the same time, was angry and vengeful. The face, if you can call it a face, was kind of human but not human. It was kind of like a goat, sort of a bear, whose face was sliced by a hatchet. It had the expression of a dead body, all rotten and jelly-like. The face of whatever it was smeared into the ice and was glaring right at the boys. There were purple scars with maggots and blood oozing from its squashed nose. The eyes were out of the sockets and bulged as if they were coming right out of the ice. There was a green glowing slime everywhere, and the eyeballs stared at the boys. A pungent smell seemed to be seeping up from the ice—a smell not unlike an old outhouse.

Just then, a loud moaning voice beckoned from the grotesque face, "Children, children, come here children." The two could not take their eyes off the monstrous form. The more they stared, the brighter the face became, and then it started to move. At the same moment, an unearthly bellow erupted from beneath the ice, "Children, children, now I have children!"

"Let's get out of here," Frankie shrieked as he bolted toward the shore, with Burt close behind. The boys ran and never looked back. They fell a few times on the ice but jumped up and kept running. They ran the whole way home and didn't even stop at the iceboat shed for their Sunday clothes.

A long time later, after facing the local police and their very angry parents; hauling the heavy iceboat across the river by themselves while being lectured by their irate father; watching as a shiny new padlock was placed on the door of the iceboat house; hearing a sermon from their dad that was twice as long as Reverend Forman's had ever been; and eating supper at a silent dinner table and being sent to their room while the family had dessert, Frankie and Burt sat quietly, staring out their bedroom window at the Navesink.

"Dad says the boat is damaged and we won't be doing any iceboating this winter," Burt sighed.

"Yeah, and they had coconut custard pie for dessert. That is my favorite," Frankie answered.

"Yeah, I know," Burt said. "But we did see it."

"I know, but no one believes us." Frankie walked to the window and opened it, allowing a gust of cold air into the room. The icy breeze brought a peculiar stench. "That stinks; close the window," Burt ordered. Frankie looked out onto the frozen Navesink. Just as he did, a single, lonely iceboat glided downriver, its white sail reflected by the full moon. The face of the pilot was unusually large and seemed to cast a green glow. Frankie was certain he heard someone laugh and call out, "Children, children, I want children."

7
THE OYSTER WARS

D id you know that there was once a war fought on the Navesink and Shrewsbury Rivers? It's true. It was known as the Oyster War. It was a series of battles over a small mollusk, *Crassostrea virginica*, or the eastern oyster. Although the details of this conflict are not common knowledge, there is significant documentation of the lengthy legal and, sometimes, violent skirmishes that arose along the river.

The Navesink natives had harvested oysters for hundreds of years before the European settlers arrived. The protein-rich oysters quickly became popular across the colonies and became a mainstay of the colonial diet. Soon, there was demand for oysters in nearby New York City. Using the Navesink as a highway, sailing sloops and schooners transported oysters by the bushel down the river and across the bay to the city. Before long, the little mollusks became a local specialty. Independent watermen, as well as local farmers with waterfront property, harvested oysters and shipped them from the Red Bank docks. So great was the demand that by the later part of the 1700s, many of the natural oyster beds were nearly depleted. Farmers with land touching the shoreline began importing oyster stock and planting them in the water, allowing them to mature before harvest.

In the early eighteenth century, oyster planting was a lucrative business. Even in colonial times, arguments arose over the oyster beds. Those who planted the oysters claimed the rights to the oyster beds on their waterfront property, while the independent oystermen insisted that the river was public property and was open to all. Colonial New Jersey regulated a specific season for harvesting oysters and restricted harvest to genuine residents of the colony. After the Revolution, the new state supported the right of farmers to private access to the oysters from their own shoreline.

In the early 1800s, two oystermen were arrested harvesting one thousand oysters from a bed planted by a local farmer. They were required to pay a restitution of three dollars for their deed. The oystermen appealed the ruling and, with the support of many local watermen, took the case to the New Jersey Supreme Court in February 1808. The case polarized the local communities. The farmers demanded that the state uphold the existing regulation of the planters' rights to the water adjacent to their land. The watermen, however, reiterated their claim that the waterways cannot be owned and that they were free to collect oysters anywhere in the Navesink, as it was public property. Local newspapers took the side of the planters and referred to the watermen as pirates and poachers.

Court cases sprouted up everywhere, but so did the raids of the planted oyster beds. Because the Navesink is a brackish estuary, the "river pirates" refused to acknowledge that the waterway was anything but common property of the people. The planters fought back to protect their investment, and the "pirates" fought to maintain their livelihood. The situation was made more complicated by the fact that the state did sell leases to the planters in other similar waterways in and around the state. For political reasons, this was never done in the Navesink or Shrewsbury. So, the battle continued.

When shotgun diplomacy failed to quell the problem, violence resulted. There were ongoing feuds, resulting in fights and actual killings. Usually, the planters were acquitted of any crime, as local authorities supported the rights of the landowners to protect their property. Planters were forced to hire armed guards to watch over their precious oyster beds. Despite the hostile climate, the raids continued. The raiders would come at night in small rowboats and tie up to the stakes the planters had imbedded into the riverbed to mark their plots. Then, they would wade into the shallow water and use oyster forks to harvest the mature oysters. When they had gathered what they could carry away in a boat, they would simply row away.

According to local lore, the Oyster War happened around the same time that Sam Higgins fell onto hard times. He knew it was his own fault—well, partly his fault. The major part of the blame went to rum. If it didn't taste so sweet and make him so sleepy, Sam would still have a full-time job. But times were tough; so, when Nathan Johnson, a Navesink planter, offered him a post as a night watchman for his oyster beds, Sam jumped at the chance. He knew Johnson was a hard taskmaster and had a reputation for being a cranky old miser. But he didn't care; he needed the money.

Harvesting oysters from a small rowboat is backbreaking work. *From Fresh and Marine Library.*

On the first evening, Johnson walked Sam to the makeshift shed by the water's edge, where he was supposed to keep watch. He gave him a lantern, some leftover meat pie from supper and an old shotgun. Sam was happy for the food, but he was a bit sad that it didn't come with liquid refreshment. Johnson mumbled a litany of instructions that included, "If you see anyone in my oyster beds, you shoot them!" Sam was an easygoing fellow and offered, "Don't you want me to just shoot over their head and scare them away?"

"No!" Johnson bristled. "Last month, there were poachers, damned water pirates, right here in my beds. One night, I caught an old fisherman right here on the bank. I know he was about to steal my oysters. He claimed he was just taking a walk at night because he had trouble sleeping. He even rattled off some old seafarer's legend. It was a bunch of superstition. When he tried to walk away, I shot him. Yep, shot him right in the back. "

"You did?"

"I sure did. Knocked him right into the water. Tide was going out, and that is the last I saw of old Jack Campbell," Johnson snickered. "I spent a lot of money replanting these plots, and they should be ready in a couple of weeks, so they need to be guarded. You got that?"

"Yes sir," Sam barked back.

As Johnson started to walk back toward the house, he stopped and turned to face Sam. "And, Sam," he said, shaking his finger, "no booze when you are working."

"Yes sir, no booze, not even a drop," Sam called after him.

It was quiet on the river that night. Sam gazed out over the glassy water and smiled to himself. He knew Old Man Johnson was sure to check up on him, but all he had to do was stay awake. The snap of twigs underfoot and the rustling of leaves brought Sam to full attention. He peered along the riverbank. Something was moving at the water's edge, and it was coming toward him. He picked up the gun and squinted to try and make out the figure. "All is well, Mr. Johnson," Sam called out. The figure paused for a moment, then continued moving closer. Samuel saw that it was not his employer but an older man, someone he didn't know.

"Hello there," the figure beckoned. "I don't mean to alarm you, sir." He reached out to shake Samuel's hand. "My name is Jack; I live upriver. I just couldn't get to sleep tonight, so I decided to take a walk." The man was obviously a seaman. He wore stained canvas pants and a wrinkled work shirt. His craggy and scarred face showed his age. But it was a friendly face, and soon, the two were chatting like old friends. Within minutes, they were calling each other Jack and Sam. Both had done some fishing in their day, and both liked woodworking. After a bit, Jack pulled out a jug from his canvas coat. He held it up so Sam could see. Both men smiled, and soon, it was like they had been friends their entire lives.

Leaning on the side of the old shed, the two passed the bottle back and forth. Jack regaled Sam with seafaring exploits, which were all tall tales, and Sam recounted his adventures traveling west, where he had never been.

It wasn't long before Sam began to yawn. "Say, mate, why don't you get some shut eye. Sleep for an hour; it will do you good." Sam started to protest, but Jack reminded him, "I've stood watch hundreds of time at sea. I know what to look for. If I see anything, I'll wake you." So, helped by the rum and the gentle waves lapping on the shore, Samuel fell asleep. It wasn't long before someone called out from the house, "Is everything okay, Sam?"

"Yes, sir, everything is fine," a calm and sober voice that sounded just like Sam answered. The lights went out in the house, and once again, it was quiet. Jack picked up a darkened lantern, walked a few feet along the shoreline and scanned the horizon. He uncovered the lantern and, in a quick motion, swept it up and down two times. He quickly covered the light, waited a few moments and repeated his movements. Within a few minutes, the sound of oars and the gentle swish of water could be heard as a small rowboat pulled up to the riverbank. Jack tipped his hat to the two men. In total silence, the men waded into the shallows. Each used a long fork-like tool and began plucking oysters from the depths. When their baskets were full, they loaded them into the boat. They tipped their hats to Jack and rowed away into the darkness.

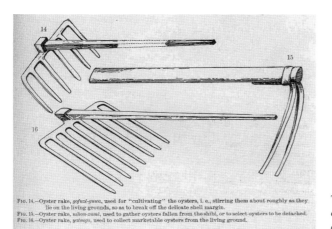

FIG. 14.—Oyster rake, *pofusé-guwa*, used for "cultivating" the oysters, i. e., stirring them about roughly as they lie on the living grounds, so as to break off the delicate shell margin.
FIG. 15.—Oyster rake, *nihon-zumé*, used to gather oysters fallen from the shibi, or to select oysters to be detached.
FIG. 16.—Oyster rake, *yatsugo*, used to collect marketable oysters from the living ground.

The tools of the oysterman. *From Fresh and Marine Library.*

For many nights afterward, Jack walked along the riverbank late in the evening to meet his friend Sam. He never came empty handed, as he always arrived with a bottle of rum. Jack told exciting yarns of the sea, and Sam chattered about his plans to someday visit California. One night, when the bottle was nearly empty, Jack asked Sam if he believed in ghosts. "Ghosts?" Sam laughed. "I'm a man who has to see it to believe it. No, I can't say I believe in ghosts. I suppose you do, you ole seadog." Sam chuckled as he took another swig from the bottle. "How many spooks have you seen?"

"Well," Jack said as he leaned over to look directly into Sam's face, "you know that mariners see things in this world that landlubbers could never hope to see."

Sam guffawed, "Go on! That's just superstition."

"Maybe so," Jack said. "I do know that when a mariner dies, his spirit returns to the place of his death, and that, my friend, is a fact. Sometimes, he comes back just to help out another seaman in need. But if the old seadog, as you call him, met a violent end, he will always come back for revenge." Jack passed the bottle to Sam once more. "Would you believe it if you saw it?" When there was no answer, he looked over and saw that Sam was fast asleep. Jack smiled.

One day, two weeks later, the planter sent his workmen to harvest the oysters, only to find that the entire bed was totally depleted. They could only find a few oysters in the entire plot. Johnson flew into a rage. He sent a worker to get Sam, telling him to bring the watchman back even if he had to hogtie him. When the farmhand described Johnson's rage, Samuel made a quick decision. He snatched his essential belongings and headed to the dock to catch the next packet out of town. As darkness fell over the Navesink that night, Jack approached the shed and saw that it was empty. He looked up to the sky and smiled. "Good for you, my friend. I hope you like California," he murmured. He took Sam's seat on the bench and sat gazing out over the water. For a while, it was quiet.

Jack knew the planter was nearby long before he saw him. The man's rage was like a stench drifting off a moss bunker left on the riverbank to rot. Johnson tore into the shed, aiming his shotgun. "I'll kill you, Sam Higgins, you miserable drunk!" When he saw that it wasn't Sam, he took a step backward, "Who in blazes are you?" he demanded.

"Just an old seaman out for a walk. I don't sleep well at night, you know."

Johnson made a gargled sound. "You?" he stammered. "You can't be Jack Campbell. I killed you when you tried to steal my oysters. I watched you float down the river with my own eyes."

"But I am here. I am the innocent man you shot in the back. I was just an aged seaman out for a walk that night. You should have listened when I tried to tell you that a mariner's spirit returns to the place where he died. It's true. Here I am."

"I don't believe it," the planter snarled.

The figure began to glow, rose slowly above Johnson's head and drifted over the shallow water. "I am here now, Norman Johnson, and I will be here always. I am the new watchman for your oyster beds. You will never harvest another oyster from this river as long as you live." With that, the figure began to spin about and plunged into the depths of the Navesink with a great splash.

Locals say that Johnson tried in vain to replant his oyster beds afterward. Each time, his harvest was for naught. Finally, deeply in debt, he sold his property and moved inland, far away from oysters and the specters that guarded them.

8

CIVIL WAR SILHOUETTE

U nlike the American Revolution, where the Navesink area was at the center of military action, during the Civil War, the Navesink region was spared any major battles. Yet, the area suffered the horrendous loss of more than seven thousand brave young men. The fifty-two regiments from New Jersey fought in battles all across the nation. The river, too, paid a toll for the war. As the war progressed, the river's commerce grew into predominately war-related materials and equipment. Mariners, as well as their vessels, were conscripted into national service. Both sailing ships and steamboats were either recruited or leased to the government. A total of thirty steamers from the northern New Jersey coast were drafted for military service between 1861 and 1865. Of these, at least six steamboats with regular Red Bank–New York routes became troop-carrying vessels. Steamers quickly became workhorses for the navy, patrolling the rivers and inlet waterways all along the East Coast and the Mississippi River.

Steamboats transported goods and troops toward the battles, and afterward, they carried the survivors, as well as the dead and wounded, away from the battle scene. After the war, the ships that were not sunk or severely damaged were returned to the river. A few, with a fresh coat of paint courtesy of the military, resumed their original Navesink routes. For half a century after the Civil War, there were numerous reports of sightings of ghost ships on the Navesink. The similarity of the accounts over those years is quite astonishing. The sightings always occur at night, when the river is quiet. The witnesses insist that the steamboats seem to be floating on the water, moving along without the use of the engines or paddlewheels. The crafts have neither markings nor navigational lights, as if they are trying to avoid being detected.

One of the most notable accounts is derived from the journal of a local Dutch landowner named Lucas from the 1890s. His family had lived in the area since before the Revolution, and Lucas knew the river like the back of his hand. He had survived the Civil War, but some nights, the horror invaded his sleep. On these nights, he found solace sitting by the water with his journal and pipe.

The day had been hot and humid, and the night promised nothing more. Lucas leaned against a barrel on the dock that jetted into the river from his farm. He made notes in a small brown journal until the light faded away. He then turned his attention to the quiet of the dark night. Everything was so still; it was as if the heat and humidity had overpowered the river breeze. Even the tidal movement was imperceptible, leaving the river looking more like a lake.

Lucas glanced from the shore across the river. He pondered how very different it was in the daytime, with the steamboats and cargo boats hauling produce to the city. Yet, tonight, one could hardly ascertain that there was any life on the river at all. Lucas looked down as a mosquito landed on his forearm. With one loud smack, he knocked it onto the dock.

When he looked up, he noticed a faint glow on the water far upstream. It was no more than a twinkle, but Lucas found himself spellbound by the tiny flicker. He couldn't be sure at first, but it seemed that the tiny greenish light was moving downstream toward him. There was no sound, not even the flap of a paddlewheel. It was most peculiar that the greenish light didn't bob in the water like a boat; it seemed to be floating just above the waterline. As he watched, the light moved slowly and steadily downstream toward him. He walked to the edge of the dock to get a better look. He could tell that it was indeed a vessel that seemed to be drifting with the tide.

At last, the boat drew near. A greenish hue hovered over the bow, where groups of blue uniformed men sat huddled together in small groups. Some bent forward in earnest conversation, while others sat, holding their heads in their hands. A low murmur could be heard over the faint melody from a harmonica. Lucas rubbed his eyes—it couldn't be. It was Union soldiers. The war had ended over thirty years ago.

When he glanced up, he was suddenly overwhelmed with exhaustion, and uncontrolled tears trickled down his cheeks. He had no time to compose himself before the mid-deck of the steamer came into view. There, the blue forms were lying in rows across on the deck. Others sat precariously, leaning against the railing. A lone dark figure moved slowly between them, pausing for a few moments before moving on to the next. In the same instant, the harmonica's melody was replaced with guttural moans and crying. The cries of anguish grew so loud, they seemed to be coming from the river itself. Before Lucas could catch his breath, the stern came into view. There, the greenish hue faded to a sickening gray. The glow hovered over log-shaped fabric parcels that were stacked in small pyramids and stretched along the width of the steamer. As he watched, a gust of wind whipped away the covering, exposing the distorted faces of the corpses.

Lucas jerked his eyes from the scene to search for the nameplate on the ship. He gasped; it was the *Navesink*, a local steamboat named for the river that was lost in the war. It had been sunk during a skirmish in a Southern river and never returned home. For a few moments, he stood frozen in place. It was only when the ship disappeared into the darkness that the dreadful crying faded away. He had heard rumors of ghost ships on the river, but he never believed them. He scooped up his journal and hurried to the house to record his encounter.

Although Lucas never saw the phantom ship again, reports of the sightings continued for five decades. But at the advent of World War I, they suddenly ceased. They have not been seen since. Who can explain the phenomenon?

9

BEYOND THE VEIL

A VICTORIAN GHOST PARTY

The Navesink shores were bustling with activity during the Victorian age. Local businesses and industries thrived as the demand for local agricultural products mushroomed. As transportation became cheaper and easier, the shore communities not only increased in population but gained a sizeable summer tourist industry. Fashionable Victorian mansions sprouted up along the riverbanks as the populace became more urbane. Recreational and cultural activities expanded, and locals joined in the growing spiritualism movement. Local interest in ghost stories and the supernatural is evidenced by the frequent paranormal accounts published in local newspapers. Nearly every edition contained at least one advertisement for a local medium or a clairvoyant. So, it is not surprising that popular entertainment during Victorian times were ghost parties.

Although such gatherings might be compared to modern Halloween parties, there were distinct differences. These parties were elaborate social events, using formal standards of Victorian entertainment and etiquette. Although they were mostly held in the autumn, they frequently occurred anytime between early October and the New Year. Those affiliated with the spiritualist movement emphasized communication with the dead, while admittedly, others were simply social events. Victorian homes all along the Navesink, which were adorned with detailed and ornate seasonal decorations, were the sites of these elaborate events. Light from candles and small oil lamps reflected glittery lace chandelier sways and rich jewel tone draperies that flowed from ceiling to floor, gathering in great puddles of fabric.

Equally formal was the extravagant bill of fare. A Victorian hostess took great pride in her menu and table presentation. Using her best linens, the refreshments were stylishly served on her finest china, silver and crystal glassware. Sometimes, these events included a formal sit-down dinner party. Other times, great buffet tables were heaped with both hot and cold foods. Appetizers, meats, seafood, potatoes and vegetable dishes might have been served. Other times, elegant tea sandwiches, tarts, pasties and nut-filled breads graced the table. A separate, but nonetheless bountiful, dessert table could always be found. Beautiful crystal and silver serving pieces were practically buried beneath skillfully bedecked cakes, pies, eclairs, cookies and other assorted sweets. To quench the thirst of their guests, the hosts served liquors, wines, ciders and beers, as well as punch, teas and coffee.

As critical as the food was to a successful party, the entertainment was the indispensable ingredient. The entertainment was usually the purpose of the event. Sometimes the parties were masquerades, with guests arriving in sumptuous costumes and masks. Guests danced, enjoyed recitals, played parlor games and exchanged stories of their own ghostly experiences. Often, professional storytellers recounted ghost stories while colorfully clad gypsy fortunetellers wowed guests with predictions of great love affairs and huge business successes. There may have been palm readers, mediums and psychics on hand to add to the colorful event. In some of the more elegant affairs, a New York clairvoyant would conduct a séance. Invitations to such parties were highly prized. Victorians could easily measure their social status by which invitations they received. At the same time, a host measured their social status by the individual acceptances they received to their event. Parties were serious business in Victorian times.

So, it was with some trepidation that Anna finally agreed to hold a ghost party in her home along the Navesink in 1888. Anna and her husband, George, had relocated to Black Point from New England before the war. And as much as they loved their new, beautiful house on the Navesink, New England would always be their home. Anna's late husband, George, had been a prominent businessman, but that was before the war. When the hostilities broke out, he promised Anna that when the war was over, he would take her back to New England for a visit. When he volunteered for the local regiment, Anna was beside herself with worry, and when they carried him home in that wooden box from Gettysburg, she was heartbroken. Even after her formal mourning period had ended, Anna rarely participated in social events.

Her one close friend was Louisa, who was also a war widow. For a while, Louisa had been talking with Anna about the growing spiritualism movement. She brought her literature and took her to several meetings. Although Anna was skeptical, she was enthralled with the possibility of communicating with George again and began attending séances with her friend. Soon afterward, Anna and Louisa were enjoying tea on the veranda overlooking the river, when Louisa tried to persuade Anna to hold a ghost party of her own. Anna was skeptical, but Louisa insisted she had the perfect beautiful house, with a wide veranda, for such an event. She even reminded Anna of how much George had loved entertaining in the house. Before they had finished the last of their tea, they had agreed to host a ghost party. In fact, they planned a masquerade.

The following month, Anna was busier than ever preparing for the party. There were invitations to be sent, food and drink to be chosen and prepared, decorations to be gathered and entertainment to be organized. The more time she spent planning the party, the lighter her mood became. It all took her back to her days as a young bride, when she and George had first entertained in their new home. She felt content for the first time since George had died. On a warm autumn evening in late October, her riverside home took on a dreamy, gingery glow. Candles filled every window, and dozens of carved jack-o'-lanterns traced the outlines of the long, curved entrance. Inside, the entire first floor was awash in flickering lights. The buffet tables were glittering heaps of delectable treats. In one corner of the room, an actress dressed as a gypsy practiced with her crystal ball while an ensemble played softly in the background. The front parlor had been cleared for dancing, and across the marble mantel in the great room were mounds of pumpkins, gourds, ears of corn, apples and fall foliage resting amid tall pillared candles of gold and black.

Anna stood in front of the large mirror in the entranceway, inspecting her costume. She wondered aloud if she had made a poor choice. Being a lover of Vermeer's paintings, she had designed her costume after that of *The Girl with the Pearl Earring*. The painting had always been one of her favorites, yet she worried that some of her guests may not be familiar with the Dutch painter. She purchased several yards of rich gold silk and made a full-length evening coat. Beneath it, she wore a white, flowing linen sheath. Around her waist, she tied a silk royal blue scarf, and she tied a pale-gold silk scarf around her head and behind her ears. Finally, she created a wide headband from the same blue silk as her belt and layered it over the front edge of the gold scarf. It was perfect. All that remained was a pair of pear-shaped pearl earrings. She smiled to herself, satisfied with her efforts; she was ready for her guests.

Anna greeted her guests as they arrived. She was pleased to see that they had obviously taken great care and effort in choosing their attire for her masquerade. They were all superbly dressed, and their intricately detailed masks were obviously custom made. She chatted and laughed as George Washington, Benjamin Franklin and a grand duchess arrived. They were soon followed by Gainsborough's blue boy in the most luscious blue silk Anna had ever seen. Then came several Van Dyke costumes, a Monet maiden and even another Vermeer. Anna couldn't have been more pleased; her guests had truly gotten into the spirit of the party.

The chatter and laughter were suddenly interrupted by a loud, shrieking voice. Anna spun around to face the sound. The fortuneteller had abandoned her crystal ball and stood in the very center of the living room. She waved her arms in wide circles as she shrieked, "Woe, unto you who imbibe here this night. Within seven weeks and seven days, seven of those gathered here will cast off their living spirits and join the world of the departed. So says the gypsy." With that, she flung her arms about one more time and hurried back to her crystal ball. Anna took in a deep breath. This had not been in the discussion for the entertainment. She was about to go speak to the fortuneteller when she noticed that the guests were all laughing and making light of what had happened. She thought it best to leave well enough alone. The music resumed as couples hurried to the dance floor. The lively music and happy chatter drove away any concerns anyone had about the gypsy's prediction.

Anna scoured the room for Louisa, for she had not seen her since she arrived. Her eyes fixed on some white blotches mixed among the colorful costumes. As she looked more closely, she could tell that not just one, but seven guests were dressed rather plainly, in long white sheeting. They had come as ghosts. Each ghost was talking earnestly with another guest. Anna couldn't remember greeting anyone dressed in that attire. Her invitations had clearly stated "elegant masquerade." She knew all her guests by name and could not imagine how anyone, let alone seven guests, would display such a breach of etiquette. Just as she moved toward one of the ghostly figures, a frigid breeze stung her cheeks. Startled, Anna stopped in her tracks. Just then, one of the ghosts brushed against her without pausing to excuse himself. Instead, she heard a low chuckle in her ear. Then, he disappeared among the dancers. For a moment, she lost her breath. She said aloud, "I know that laugh. Why can't I place it?"

Just then, an old friend named Florence tugged at her sleeve. "Oh, Anna, you do invite the most fascinating people to your parties," she said in a happy whisper. "Who is the gentleman who came in that simplistic ghost costume? He is so knowledgeable. We talked all about the sailing ships, like my father used to captain. He recounted such wonderful tales. It was like he had once been aboard," she said excitedly. "Who is he? I must know." Anna told her that she was unsure but that Florence would find out when they unmasked at midnight. Florence scanned the crowd. "Well, I don't want to lose sight of him. I must know who he is," she tittered as she headed into the crowd.

She had only taken a few steps when Samson and Delilah approached her. "Ah," she said, "I see that you two came as a Van Dyke." Anna knew immediately it had to be George's friend Charles and his wife, Margaret. Only Margaret would think of such a creative costume. Samson leaned forward and spoke earnestly in Anna's ear, "Where do you find such fascinating and interesting young chaps? We spoke with a most delightful young man—so enthusiastic, and he loves bicycle racing, just like our Benjamin." With that, his wife put her hand on his arm. "Please dear, I cannot bear to discuss Benjamin at a social engagement. He has only been gone two years." The man gulped and smiled weakly as he led his wife away.

Anna felt her stomach tighten. There was something going on. Just then, Louisa appeared. "Anna, I didn't know you invited others that were not on the invitation list we drew up, but I am so glad that you did. I met the most interesting man. Not only is he charming, but he has been telling the most delightful tales." She paused and sighed, "You know, in some ways, he reminds me of my husband, Mark." Although Anna tried to interrupt, Louisa chatted on, "I can't wait for the unmasking. I do want to meet him formally."

"Louisa, I need to talk with you!" Before Louisa could protest, Anna led her to the far side of the room. She recounted the seven ghost guests who she didn't remember greeting. She told her of her encounters with Florence and the couple dressed as Samson and Delilah. When she finished, Louisa gave her a quick embrace. "You worry too much; everyone is having a fabulous time. The ghosts are probably some of the men from the boating club playing a prank. It's nothing to be worried about. Go enjoy your own party." With that, she hurried back into the throng of partygoers. But something wasn't right; Anna could feel it.

The dancing was in full swing, and the merrymakers were having a wonderful time, eating, chatting and dancing. Laughter could be heard throughout the house and across the large porch. As Anna gazed across

An uninvited guest enjoys the ghost party. *From* Begger Bensen *by George Miles 1886, via the British Library.*

the room, she noticed that each ghost was once again conversing with another guest. She heard the grandfather clock strike midnight; it was time to announce the unmasking. She made her way over to the bandleader and whispered in his ear. The music softened until it was a soothing background for the announcement. With great fanfare, he announced that it was time for the unmasking dance. He called for everyone to come draw near and form two circles. Anna watched as her guests gathered in the center of the dance floor. Something made her turn and look back toward the front door. She drew in a long, deep breath, as each ghost had taken the arm of a guest and was leading them outside. As she watched, Florence, Samson and Delilah and even Louisa vanished onto the porch.

Just then, someone snatched Anna's sleeve and pulled her onto the dance floor. The inner circle was mostly composed of women, while men formed the larger outer circle. When the music began, they joined hands and began spinning around. The inner circle danced to the right, and the outer circle danced to the left. The music grew faster, and at last, it reached a crescendo. Shouts of "Unmask!" echoed throughout the house. Masks were peeled away and cast aside. People shrieked in recognition and laughter. At once, the music resumed, and the dance floor was filled with swirling couples.

When Anna finally made her way through the crowd to the porch, she found that the ghosts and their partners were gone. Soon afterward, the guests began departing. There was a jumble as carriages were called for and farewells were exchanged. By the time Anna returned to the porch, everyone had gone. Louisa, too, was nowhere to be found. Although Anna found Louisa's behavior unusual, she decided that Louisa must have been feeling tipsy and accepted a carriage ride with a friend.

When all the guests had departed, Anna gave final cleaning instructions to the staff and announced she was going to bed. As she started up the stairs, she caught something out of the corner of her eye, something white. Standing near George's pipe collection was one of the guests still in his ghost costume. Anna hurried back down the stairs and approached him. "Excuse me, I didn't realize you were still here. We have all unmasked some time ago. You should—"

Before she could utter another word, a low, hoarse voice whispered, "You really don't know who I am, do you?" And then, he laughed, not a snicker or mere chuckle, but a loud, booming laugh that echoed off the walls of the house. The cleaning crew took no notice of the loud laughter. Anna gasped. She knew that laugh—that booming laugh—could only belong to one man, her husband, George.

The next morning, the maid found Anna, still in her costume, propped up in her bed. Her eyes were closed, and though she was certainly dead, her face was peaceful and relaxed. In her hand, she clutched her diary with her final entry: "George finally came to take me home."

It has been said that six others from the party passed away or simply vanished within seven weeks and seven days of the party, but no one knows for certain, as no one is willing to speak of it.

10
THE GHOST AT THE GREEK CLUB

Despite sub-zero temperatures and relentless icy winds off the Navesink, the Christmas season was in full swing in December 1922. The storefronts and shop windows were clad in bright red and green, anxious to welcome shoppers. Men held their fedoras tightly and women clutched their parcels against their coats. Town was bustling as residents attempted to make the most of these last few shopping days before Christmas. Few took notice of a short article in the *Daily Register* on December 20. It was a single-column piece hidden far from the front page. Buried deep within the advertisements for holiday gifts and treats, it detailed a curious incident at the Red Bank Greek Club on Broad Street.

The Monmouth Refurbishing and Cleaning Company was owned by a popular Greek merchant named George Noglows. His Haddon Building Shop catered to gentlemen clientele and specialized in the cleaning and care of hats, as well as shoe care and repair. His success grew from his serious and practical approach to business, his civic involvement and his friendly nature. Like the majority of people in the early twentieth century, George did not believe in ghosts, but that was about to change.

On the second floor, above his shop, the Greek Club maintained a fellowship room. All the members were Greek immigrants who gathered to play dominoes and cards and share a drink or two with their countrymen. Occasionally, it also served as a bedroom in the event a member had too much to drink and needed to sleep it off. In early December, a well-liked club member named Louis Caras was killed in an accident. Members of the Greek Club were saddened and frequently met to reminisce about their old friend. They agreed that the club just wasn't the same without him.

One night was particularly frigid, with temperatures hovering around zero. The Greek Club was not meeting that night, so George permitted his young shoeshine boy, Gus, to stay overnight in the clubroom instead of walking the mile and a half home in the cold. Gus readily agreed and happily snuggled that night beneath the quilts in the small bed. Around 2:00 a.m., Gus suddenly awoke. The room was dark and silent, but Gus felt as if someone was there. "Who's there?" he called. "Mr. Noglows, is that you?" There was no answer. The room remained silent and dark. The only sound Gus could hear was the beating of his own heart. As he pulled the covers up around his chin, the ceiling light suddenly flashed on. Gus choked down a scream. He was shaking so badly he couldn't hold the blankets in his hands. Wrapping the quilt around himself, he reached for the iron poker in the fireplace. Ever so slowly, he searched the entire room. There was no one there. As he returned to his bed, the lights flashed off, leaving him in the darkness. Gus shrieked in fright, pulled on his shoes and, without even grabbing his coat, ran the entire way home.

When Gus reported the events to George the following morning, George couldn't believe his ears. He had always thought Gus was a mature lad and was truly surprised that the boy was so emphatic about what had happened. Attempting to make light of the situation, George chuckled, "Well, maybe it's just a ghost." But Gus didn't want to talk about it and insisted that he would never sleep there again. So, George promised Gus he would sleep there himself that very night.

After the store closed, George took his supper up to the room. He ate leisurely as he reviewed the day's accounts. He made a point to be certain that the windows and door were securely locked. Then, he crept into the bed and fell asleep. Around 2:00 a.m., George was awakened when the lights in the room flashed on. After his initial startle, he inspected the room. Finding nothing amiss, he crawled back into bed. Thinking someone was playing a joke on him, he laughed out loud and turned off the lights. A few minutes later, another light flashed on. George got out of bed and turned that light off. He had just gotten back into bed when it happened again. Every time George turned one light off, another turned itself on. George was a practical man; he was convinced his pals were playing tricks on him.

Despite his attempts to figure out how the joke had been accomplished, he waited out the night and, in the morning, called for an electrician to come and inspect the wiring in the room. The electrician smiled as he handed George the bill. "There is nothing wrong with the electricity in that room, but I still have to charge you." George was more convinced than ever that his buddies from the club were playing pranks on him and decided to play along. That night, he returned to sleep in the clubroom. As usual, it was quiet until around 2:00 a.m. Then, once again, the lights started to misbehave. George called out, "Come in. I'd like to speak with you. You are welcome here." There was no response. "Can I offer you a drink?" he asked, holding a bottle in the air. Even then, there was no response. The lights flashed on and off a few more times and then stopped. George laughed and drifted off to sleep, wondering how his friends had managed the hoax.

The next morning, George cheerfully sought out his friends to learn who had pulled such a complicated stunt. They all denied it and began teasing him about being haunted. George began checking the room repeatedly. Nothing happened in the daytime, but each night, around 2:00 a.m., the same events repeated. The lights would come on and then suddenly turn themselves off. When the nightly episodes continued, George persuaded three friends to spend the night in the clubroom with him. One lightheartedly insisted that George should bring his gun. The four men sat in the darkness, smoking cigars and waiting; 2:00 a.m. came and went, but nothing happened.

George's friends began to tease him mercilessly. The three men were

The men of the Greek Club bolted into the street when visited by the ghost. *From A. Rackham, www. oldbookillustrations.com.*

laughing uncontrollably when the darkness was ripped away; every light in the room suddenly flashed on. At the same moment, a cloudlike face appeared at the window. George grabbed his gun and fired, but nothing happened—the gun misfired. Then, the lights snapped off. The four men practically knocked one another over trying to escape the room. Chairs, tables and pictures were tossed about everywhere.

They ran down Broad Street until they found a beat cop and brought him back to the room. They stuttered in dismay at what they saw. The room, which they had left in such disorder, was now neat and orderly, with the furniture in its original position. On the bed lay a spent bullet. The bullet was distorted as if it had hit something, but no damage could be found anywhere in the room.

The next day, Detective Sergeant Joseph Bray inspected the scene and found no evidence of either an intruder or the damage from a shooting. After the newspaper reported the incident, George was deluged with curious visitors wanting to visit the room and offers to exorcise it—for the right price. George took it all in good humor, and finally, interest in the specter died down. Today, we are left to wonder if the current residents of the property have been graced by the ghost of the Greek Club or if Louis Caras just wanted to say hello to his friends one more time.

11
DUBLIN HOUSE

THE HOUSE THAT CROSSED A RIVER

Many of the great old residences in the Navesink area are said to be haunted, so it isn't surprising that a nineteenth-century mansion with a history like the Dublin House in Red Bank would have active paranormal activity. Not only does the building have a resident ghost but it has a phantom that has been witnessed by both staff and patrons. It is not a random haunting for sure; the Dublin House phantom is none other than its former mistress, Roberta Patterson.

The adventures of the house began in 1840, when it was uprooted from its foundation in Middletown and floated across the Navesink on a barge. Little is known about it before it was purchased by Robert Allen Jr., who moved it once again. This time, its destination was the west side of Broad Street. There, at 60 Broad Street, the small home underwent a massive renovation, which included the addition of a second and third floor. The addition of unique architectural alterations resulted in the beautiful Mansardic mansion we know today as the Dublin House.

Robert Allen Jr., a prominent lawyer, real estate developer and member of the New Jersey Legislature, supervised the transformations of his home with a sharp eye. He lived in the house with his wife and two daughters until his death in 1903. After his death, the house was inherited by his eldest daughter, Roberta Allen Patterson. Roberta and her husband, George Hance Patterson, moved the larger, newly renovated house yet again. This time, the task to move the mansion was more complicated. At last, in 1905, the mansion came to rest in its current location at 30 Monmouth Street. The

The Dublin House in Red Bank, New Jersey, is a modern restaurant with a resident ghost. *Photograph by author.*

couple spent the remainder of their lives there. Mr. Patterson died in 1938, and his wife lived for many more years in the house before passing away in 1953. As the couple had no children, Roberta Patterson's estate was left to her nephew and two nieces.

It was some time before the estate was settled, but by 1971, the building was commercial property. This was a new era for the old house. A series of businesses called the mansion home. As the "House on Monmouth Street," it held a number of shops, including an ice cream parlor, chocolate and candle stores, two gift shops and a restaurant. Other short-term businesses in the house included Longfellow's, Whiskers and El Parador. A coffeehouse, too, once occupied part of the second floor.

People have claimed that the Dublin House is haunted for many years. During the 1960s, youngsters approached the house with trepidation. Claims were made that a ghostly figure lived in the old house. After it became commercial property, the allegations continued. Upstairs, in the coffeehouse, the coffee would sometimes brew all by itself. In the other shops, lights would turn on and off, doors would slam and strawberry ice cream would frequently be lobbed off tables.

In the late 1980s, the Dubliner Pub, which did business farther down the street, moved to 30 Monmouth Street with great fanfare. A parade of patrons and staff from the pub marched up Monmouth Street to officially open the Dublin House. In 2004, the pub was purchased by two Irish restaurateurs who had new plans for the house. Realizing the building had been neglected and poorly renovated over the years, they undertook a massive rehabilitation and restoration project to restore the building to its former glory. This was not an easy or inexpensive venture, as the house was sinking and in desperate need of major infrastructural work.

During the early days of renovation, the resident ghost seemed rather annoyed by all the noise and dust. She made her presence known by knocking over walls and equipment at will. It took some time for the ghost to become acclimated with Dunne and Devlin's renovation, but once she saw their determination to repair and preserve the beauty of the house, she seemed to be pleased with the arrangement.

The owners acknowledge her presence, happily greeting her each morning. Although some days go by without contact between the ghost and humans, other days are filled with interactions. She frequently unlocks doors and turns lights on and off. She likes a tidy household and has been known to organize a messy desk or rearrange items that are out of place in the restaurant.

The resident ghost sometimes shows her mischievous side by sliding a bottle off the bar late at night. Other times, she follows patrons and waitresses around the restaurant. Roberta is known to love music. Every night, the staff turns the radio system off at closing, but frequently, music is playing when they arrive in the morning. Both staff and patrons mostly report amicable experiences with the ghost.

One patron, however, reported an auditory experience with a highly peeved Mrs. Patterson during the autumn of 2012. She was alone in the ladies' room when she heard a harsh, irritated voice complaining about the "damned kids" who leave the bathroom messy. The tirade went on for some time. When the voice grew more agitated, the patron quickly washed her hands and fled the room.

When Devlin and Dunne purchased the building, they discovered it came with its very own local historian, T.J. McMahon. As a regular at the Dublin House, he spent many hours sharing his knowledge of the mansion's history and especially its ghostly mistress. After his passing in 2005, the Dublin House dedicated the downstairs dining room to his memory. An assortment of T.J. McMahon's works, photos and memorabilia are displayed in a large wooden display cabinet mounted on the far wall. On one occasion a few years ago, just as a family was leaving their table beneath the case, it came crashing down to the floor. No one was injured, but the case was broken, and its contents were scattered about. The case was repaired and securely bolted to the studs to prevent any further problems. The memorabilia was carefully arranged so that a framed portrait of McMahon faced the room. Once closed, it was secured with special screws so that the case could not be opened without great difficulty. The next morning, when staff arrived, the photo of McMahon was facing the wall. Since it was impossible for anyone to open the cabinet, it was agreed that only Mrs. Patterson could have turned the picture toward the wall. Apparently, she was displeased with the historian's constant discussion of the details of her family's life. The case remains unchanged in respect for her wishes.

So, what does a modern business do when it has a resident ghost? Rather than flee from the idea, the Dublin House has welcomed and embraced its resident spirit. Although the owners already knew they had a ghost, paranormal investigators have verified the existence of spirit in the building. The Dublin House ghost exhibits distinct maternal qualities. Just as any mother, she watches over the house and its occupants. At times, she gets annoyed with those around her, and sometimes, just like any mother, she is mischievous and teases patrons with evidence of her presence.

The cordial relationship between the owners and their resident spirit may be the result of circumstance and coincidence. Mrs. Patterson never had children. As she grew older, surely, there may have been times she wished she had a son to help her care for the old house. She didn't need just any son; she needed a son who would love the old mansion as she did. Devlin and Dunne filled that niche. She has not one but two sons who respect and care for her home. They lovingly maintain and respect the great house and fill it daily with laughter, good food and comradery. With people around all the time, she can never be lonely. What more could a motherly ghost want? It is not surprising that she stays.

If you stop off at the Dublin House, feel free to greet her and invite her to pull up a chair or sit beside you at the bar. Who knows? You might meet her, too.

12

CONUNDRUM AT LOGGY HOLE FARM

Situated along the wetlands of the Shrewsbury River and extending along the Sycamore Avenue section of modern-day Shrewsbury and Little Silver Streets lies a 112-acre plot of land that was once known as Loggy Hole Farm. The farm no longer exists, as it was replaced long ago by housing developments and businesses. Yet, as early as 1838, the homestead had already gleaned its curious name, and rumors circulated of peculiar happenings on the property. Although the farm exchanged hands many times over the years, its multiple owners retained the name Loggy Hole Farm well into the twentieth century. The area remained sparsely populated, with land usage being primarily agricultural. But in the early 1800s, the farm entered a century-long encounter with a series of bizarre and inexplicable events.

We know that Loggy Hole Farm was well-known and successful throughout the years, despite both its unattractive name and the growing number of reported peculiar events happening there. By 1892, Loggy Hole Farm had been sold once again. This time, the farm belonged to E.C. Hazard, a local businessman who owned both a wholesale food distribution company and a recently acquired tomato canning business, which was also located in Shrewsbury. Within a few short years, Loggy Hole Farm became the center of his large vegetable canning business. By the 1890s, Shrewsbury Ketchup was a popular condiment found on tables across the region.

Why would any landowner burden his property with such an unattractive name? Some say the name is Dutch in origin, while others claim that part of the property is adjacent to the wetlands and is marshy and somewhat bog-like. Since we do not know who named the farm or their rationale for doing so, it remains another part of the mystery that surrounds the property.

We do know, however, that documents from the 1860s mention the existence of quicksand on the site. Early colonists were warned of quicksand pits by the Lenape. Those who did not heed the warning often discovered it themselves—sometimes, with tragic consequences. By the beginning of the Civil War, many quicksand pockets had already been mapped. The conundrum of Loggy Hole Farm does not lie with the quicksand issue alone. But when this is combined with a series of baffling paranormal events on the property, one is left with a most peculiar puzzle.

During the mid-1800s, Loggy Hole Farm was a bustling and successful homestead. With its sizable labor force, it produced an assortment of fruits and vegetables and served as a facility for breeding both cattle and horses. It was also a common practice for a farm to keep a kennel of hunting hounds,

The hounds of Loggy Hole were enticed to disaster by a gray phantom creature. *From www. pixabay.com.*

and Loggy Hole Farm was no exception. Its hounds were known to be some of the best in the area.

One gray morning, Milton Geist, the farmhand who had the sole responsibility of caring for the dogs, finished feeding the hounds and opened the gate to the outside fenced kennel, which was connected to their enclosed shelter. The dogs bounded into the fresh air and began running about, playfully nipping at one another. Milton was cleaning the inside shelter when he first heard a low whimpering sound coming from the dogs that quickly escalated into growls, snarls and, finally, the distinctive bay of hunting dogs.

Milton turned toward the sound of the ruckus just in time to see the pack leader, General, throw his body against the outside gate. The spring catch snapped, and General bounded out of the kennel with the entire pack of hounds on his heels. The dogs bolted away, racing toward the outer pasture and the river. Milton shouted but to no avail. He jumped on a barrel to see where they were headed, just in time to see the pack chasing a smoky gray animal along the outer fence line. He squinted to get a better look at the creature the dogs were chasing. He saw a silvery gray body with a long snout just inches ahead of the pack. He looked again; it was certainly not a common red fox, which are known to inhabit the area. It was grayish, almost white. But Milton knew it couldn't be a wolf, as it lacked the profile and distinctive wolf-like head.

The creature darted through the outer fence, followed by the pack of hounds nipping at its tail. Milton gasped and began running as fast as his legs could carry him. The dogs were headed toward the river and the quicksand mire on the far edge of the farm. By the time he reached the quagmire, the silvery invader had disappeared. Instead, he found several dogs thrashing about at the edge of the quicksand. He pulled a few hounds to safety, but the dog in the center of the mire, the owner's prize dog, General, thrashed about frantically, unable to free himself until he was gone. Milton immediately reported the incident to the foreman, and a search was made to find and kill the intruder. When it was not found, Milton was accused of drinking on the job. Despite his claims of innocence, he was promptly fired. Although life was soon back to normal on Loggy Hole Farm, rumors began to circulate of strange lights near the river's edge and of glowing orbs floating near the quagmire. A few farmhands claimed to have seen ashen-colored animals along the exterior fence line, and once, a pet goat simply disappeared.

Monmouth County flourished in the 1890s, and Loggy Hole Farm enjoyed the prosperity. By early April 1894, Loggy Hole Farm had increased its herd of horses and had begun breeding quality animals for sale. One of the prized horses was a chestnut mare named Bernadette. She was a beautiful horse with a friendly disposition and fine muscular features. The last time she was seen alive, she had been out in the outer pasture, happily munching on the new sprouts of sweet grass. Although the mare was quiet and calm, a larger gray horse pranced and circled around her, frequently lifting his nose and snorting. Then, the larger horse began to nip at the mare, and she began darting about in a circle, trying to escape. No matter which direction she ran in, the gray horse cut her off, and she had to retreat. William, the caretaker's son, stood watching the horses for a few minutes. Although he was only nine, he had been around farm animals his whole life and he knew something wasn't right. He hurried into the barn where his father was putting down fresh hay for the animals.

"Pa," he said, "that big gray horse is chasing Bernadette all around the field."

"What are you talking about, boy? Bernadette is always in the pasture alone now; you know she is about to foal." But William insisted that a large gray horse was chasing the pregnant mare. Pa dropped his hay rake and ran toward the pasture. When he reached the gate, it stood wide open; the pasture was empty, and Bernadette was gone. The caretaker scoured the nearby field for the mare. In the distance, he thought he saw her disappear through the outer fence and into the wetlands with a large gray horse nipping at her hindquarters. He shouted for help, and instantly, half a dozen farmhands joined the chase. When they reached the outer enclosure, they could see where the horses had crashed through the fencing. They were headed toward the river, toward the swampy area near the quicksand cavity. When they reached the morass, the gray horse had disappeared. The mare, however, thrashed and struggled as the mud enveloped her within moments. She was unable to utter a sound. Despite an intense search of the property, the gray horse was never seen again.

Word quickly spread of the phantom beasts that seemed to be luring helpless animals to their deaths. Attempts were made to fill the quicksand with logs and rocks but to no avail. A strong railing was placed around the marsh, and workers were cautioned to stay out of the area. For almost ten years, there was little evidence recorded of mysterious happenings, aside from the occasional claim of seeing what looked like birds with silvery-gray wings flying in the darkness and reports of strange lights glowing over the mire. There were occasional lost pets, and once, there was a report of a missing drunken farmhand.

By 1926, machinery had come to Loggy Hole. A shiny new Farmall tractor was the pride of the farm. The farmhand with sole responsibility for the new machine could not have been happier. Fred considered himself the luckiest man alive when the foreman gave him the job. He kept the tractor in perfect working order and lovingly washed it down every evening; he even had a pet name for it, Fanny, although he never told the other workers.

One spring day, he was moving the tractor across the farm from one field to another when he saw a young girl with long, flowing hair and a blue bonnet running in a nearby field. It was unusual to see children out in the crop fields. He knew everyone in the family, most of their visitors, and certainly all the crew and their families. But he didn't recognize the little girl.

He slowed the tractor to an idle and watched the child running along the outer fence near the river. That isn't good he thought, that little one shouldn't be so near the swamp. He shouted a warning to her, but it was drowned out by the noise of the tractor motor.

She stood by the gate for a moment and seemed to stare at Fred. Then she reached up, unattached the gate and disappeared into the scrub grass on the edge of the swamp. He knew he couldn't catch her if he ran, so he put the tractor into high gear and bounced across the pasture as fast as he could. The wind lashed his face as he tried to reach the girl before she entered the wetlands. He thought he saw her blue bonnet just ahead, but then the girl suddenly disappeared. He drove the tractor a bit farther through the low shrubs. Looking around, he shouted out to her, but there was no answer.

At that moment, he felt the two small front tires of the tractor slide into muddy slime. Fred gasped; he had driven into the quicksand. The Farmall began to slide, and within moments the motor had died. Fred leapt from the sinking tractor, landing just along the edge of the quicksand. He hit hard, his right knee spouting blood. He looked across the quagmire and watched as the beautiful new tractor began to sink into the sludge. Soon just the tip of giant back tires was still in sight. He scanned the area for the child, but she was gone. When he reported the incident, his boss insisted he had been drinking and maintained that there were no little girls playing in the fields. The next day Fred went looking for a new job.

We must admit that the events at Loggy Hole Farm are not unique, but they do remain perplexing, a puzzle, indeed a conundrum. Is it some form of haunting, a shape changer, a demonic presence or a curse on the land? Or is it something else?

Who is to say what may be going on within the housing developments that grace what was once Loggy Hole Farm? Where are the missing pets? Why do residents call authorities to complain of peculiar lights in the sky and grayish shadows along the waterfront? Is it swamp gas or some other natural phenomenon? Or do the spirits that plagued Loggy Hole Farm linger still?

13

THE GRAVEYARD SHIFT AT THE OCEANIC BRIDGE

Just before the turn of the century, the original Oceanic Bridge was built, connecting Locust Point with Rumson. It was an iron and wood-planked structure with a pivot draw and a gray latticework frame that ran the length of the movable span. On each end of the river, iron and wood docks reached toward the middle of the river, where they connected on each side of the moveable pivot. The 123-foot-long moveable part rotated on a central supporting axis ring with a center tower, which rose high above the water, resting on a kind of artificial island. A turntable connected to a series of gears, clutches and wedges enabled the bridge to be rotated ninety degrees manually. The central tower housed the tender's station, which enabled the tender to both operate the mechanism and keep watch for vessels.

There were mishaps on the bridge shortly after it opened in 1891. The first happened when a local man rode his bicycle off the end of the bridge into twelve feet of water. Reports say he had downed a few pints that evening before starting for Middletown on this bike. In 1893, the schooner *Emma Hendrix* rammed the bridge on a foggy morning. The tender didn't hear the warning whistle from the boat and said that the fog was so heavy he couldn't see the ship. The bridge was unscathed, although the steamer suffered considerable damage.

The most peculiar story is one that was divulged by a young man and his uncle, an assistant bridge tender. The night was cold, and it was drizzling rain when Jim and his Uncle Pete reached the tender's box. Jim had been there many times before, of course, but he was always there to take Uncle

The Oceanic Bridge opens to allow a steamship to travel up the Navesink River. *From a vintage postcard.*

Pete some supper or watch one of the large steamboats go upriver. So, when his uncle invited him to sit the graveyard shift with him, Jim was delighted. By the time his uncle had checked the logbook, adjusted the gear mechanism and refilled the oil in the lamps, the drizzle had grown into a downpour. By 11:30 p.m., it was a full-blown gale. The water had been blown into a frenzy by the winds, and the rain hammered the tender box.

"It's nearly midnight," Jim's uncle said. "Are you getting hungry?" Before Jim could answer, Pete swore under his breath. "I left our supper in the shed on the dock." He grabbed his yellow slicker and fastened the hood snugly around his chin. "You stay here; there won't be any traffic tonight. I'll be back in a jiff." He slammed the door behind him and slowly made his way to the shed on the far bank. Jim had never been alone on the bridge before, especially not during a storm. He felt uneasy but knew his uncle was right; there would be no traffic that night. All they had to do was stay there until morning. Jim peered down the dock, hoping to see Pete returning with the food, but all he could see was darkness. The wind roared up the river and through the girders, and Jim was certain he felt the entire bridge shake.

To calm his nerves, Jim studied the inside of the tender's station. In the dim glow of the lantern, the emergency horns and beacons hung on the wall, ready for action. There were two wooden stools, a desk and the mechanism panel for rotating the span. He looked back to the shore—still no sign of his uncle. The rain pounded against the window as Jim stood with his face pressed against the glass and gazed upriver. At first, he saw only darkness; then, something glimmered in the distance. Something yellow bobbed in the water upstream. He stared at the object but couldn't make it out. He knew it couldn't have been a vessel, as someone would have to be crazy to be on the river on a night like this.

The goosebumps and the strange chill would not leave him. He peered anxiously to the shore—still no Uncle Pete. He snatched the binoculars from their hook and scanned the river. There was something there all right, something big. Jim couldn't take his eyes off the yellow bobbing object. There was definitely something there, and it was moving. He leaned against the glass for a better look. Yes, it was headed straight for the bridge. The uneasy feeling became a loud thumping. Jim knew it wasn't the rain striking the window; it was the thumping of his heart. He stared frantically toward shore—still no Pete. "Where could he be?"

The object was close enough now that Jim could see that it was an old chipped and weathered schooner. There was no evidence of a crew, and it was dark except for a yellowish glow that seemed to be escaping the cabin. He wondered what to do. Grabbing a warning lantern, he began waving it frantically. There was no response from the ship. He blew a warning blast from the distress whistle. Again, there was no response. Finally, he stepped out into the storm and shouted, "Bridge to vessel, the bridge is closed—the bridge is closed!" There was still no response from the schooner. Jim ran back inside. Did he dare open the bridge? He had seen Uncle Pete do it one hundred times, but could he do it? He had no choice; the boat was nearly on him. Lightning flashed as he depressed the T-bar into the mechanism socket. There was a scraping sound as the gears, clutches and wedges began to push against the turntable. It seemed like the bridge was not going to budge, and then, ever so slowly, the great frame began to swivel. The wind whipped against the span, and Jim felt the entire bridge rock. The bridge slowly swung into its open position.

The ship didn't hesitate. In an instant, it sailed through the opening, never once acknowledging the tender. Jim pulled the binoculars up to his face to find the nameplate on its stern; it was the *Laura Maps*. Within moments, it had sailed into the darkness. The bridge vibrated uncontrollably in the wind. Jim had to close it again before it was damaged. Ignoring the cold sweat that ran down his face, he tried to picture exactly how Pete would close the span. He inserted the bar once again, and the gears and clutches began to work; the bridge moved ever so slowly back into position. It made contact with the docks on each end and closed with a thud. It was then he saw his uncle on the far dock. He was jumping up and down, waving his arms. His uncle took time to check the locking mechanism before sprinting across the span and racing into the tender box. His face was red, and his eyes were bulging. "What do you think you are doing?" He shrieked, "How dare you risk damaging the bridge? You could get me fired!"

"I had to; that ship would have rammed the bridge." Jim blurted, "I tried to warn her but—"

"Ship? What ship?" Pete's voice was a squawk. "I didn't see a ship."

"It was the schooner, the *Laura Maps*," Jim said.

The color drained from Pete's face. "What? Did you say the *Laura Maps*?"

"Yes, I read her nameplate—the *Laura Maps*."

"Jim, it couldn't have been the *Laura Maps*. She sunk off this spot years ago. It was a night just like this." His voice trailed off.

"What do we do?" Jim asked. "Do we put it in the logbook?"

"No," Pete said with a slight smile. "Let's just keep this between you and me—and the *Laura Maps*."

14
HAUNTINGS IN
OLD MIDDLETOWN VILLAGE

Nestled along Kings Highway is the historic village of Middletown. So much American history took place there, and numerous accounts of the paranormal thrive in the village. The site is a pristine suburban thoroughfare listed in the National Register of Historic Places. The area is dotted with beautiful homes, historic buildings, old burial plots and celebrated churches from the colonial era. Around 160 years ago, the village was quite different. Kings Highway had grown along the junction of three former native paths, and it became the widest and most heavily traveled road in the area. The small village of Middletown straddled the highway and served as the nucleus of settlement. By 1851, it consisted of about forty homes, three churches, a school, a tanner, two carriage shops, three blacksmiths, a leather and harness maker, a small boardinghouse, two stores and a tavern.

Within this historic district, there is a parcel of land that has been the site of numerous exceptionally peculiar and unexplainable events that date as far back as the early 1850s. The tract is located along Kings Highway, at the juncture of what is now New Monmouth Road, and just to the east, on Kings Highway, there was a small one-room school building.

Snuggled against the school was an old private cemetery that had fallen into disrepair. The family cemetery was a private burial spot for a prominent colonial-era family. By 1850, there were more than two dozen grave sites in the cemetery—well, that's at least how many people could see. The grave markers had not weathered well in the harsh local climate. The wind and rain had washed away most of the hand-chiseled images and lettering on the old brownstone markers. Many were leaning or had simply toppled over. Although someone occasionally came with a scythe to cut away the hay-like grass that grew among the stones, the cemetery had an unkempt appearance.

The fact that the cemetery was right beside the school didn't seem to bother anybody; at least, no one complained. The children used the cemetery as a sort of playground. They chased one another through the rows of stones, and sometimes, when the weather was hot, everyone ate their lunches while resting against the cool stone slabs. Then, there came a series of peculiar events in the 1850s—phenomena no one could quite explain. The events were discussed only in whispers at first and then not at all. The tales didn't come to light until 1893, when the *Daily Register* recounted them.

Directly behind the school and cemetery, resting well back from the roadway, was the old Dutch farmhouse, which had been there for as long as anyone could remember. Most of the village folk didn't remember the original owners. For ten years, the farm had been rented out to a farming couple with a young daughter. The wife died shortly after they arrived, leaving the farmer and the daughter to manage the farm by themselves. It was well known in the village that the old farmer had a fondness for the bottle. After losing his wife, the problem became increasingly worse. He became what was known as a "hard drinker," as he was frequently intoxicated and nearly always in a hostile and angry mood.

The daughter was a kind and generous eighteen-year-old girl who had a warm heart that endeared her to everyone in the village. She not only helped her father out in the fields, but she also managed to keep the home pleasant and comfortable. No matter how difficult the old man became, she made every effort to care for him in a gentle and loving way.

As time passed, the old man's drinking problem became worse. He became more and more offensive and difficult to manage. By then, he suffered from delirium, hallucinations and what folks called the jim jams, or uncontrollable tremors. Despite the difficulty, his daughter tried her best to take care of him without outside help from either the church or the village. No one really knows if he had ever been physically violent with his daughter before, but on one cold and rainy night, when he was very drunk, his delirium became violent. He began thrashing about the house, cursing at unseen snakes and demons that he believed were stalking him. After a while, he decided that his daughter had allowed the demons and snakes to enter the house, and he threatened to kill her if she didn't immediately remove the invaders.

No matter what she did, her father would not listen to reason. The hallucinations became worse, and he grabbed a hatchet from the woodpile and began chasing his daughter throughout the house, threatening to chop her into one hundred pieces. Sometimes, he would discontinue the chase just long enough to chop off the head of some unseen demon before resuming the pursuit of his daughter. She finally managed to reach the kitchen, where she shoved through the screened door and bounded across the porch, onto the grass. Without slowing down, she sprinted through the vegetable garden and out to the field facing the old school, shrieking at the top of her lungs all the while. Her crazed father followed her screams the whole way to the school. When she reached the school, she realized that it was empty and that there was no one there to help her. Exhausted and terrified, she ran into the cemetery and crouched behind an old grave marker.

She could hear her father ranting and raving as he stumbled over the headstones searching for her. She huddled behind a brownstone slab, hardly daring to breathe. If he found her, he would surely kill her. It began to rain, a pounding cold downpour that beat down on her face as if it, too, wanted to punish her. She shivered and pulled herself into a ball, all the while certain he could hear her chattering teeth. The deluge hammered the old man, too, sending him staggering against a large headstone. Cursing the rain, he waved the old hatchet in the air at the offending downpour. Finally, he exhausted himself and slowly staggered away from the cemetery; he made his way home to the empty house.

It was quiet in the cemetery. The girl was terrified, still uncertain if he had fallen asleep nearby or if he was lying in wait. So, she stayed there, cowering behind the tombstone all night. After a while, she fell asleep. In the early morning, a passerby noticed her nestled against the grave marker. He called for help, and she was brought to the local parsonage, where she was put into a warm bed. She never regained full consciousness and died two days later. Sadly, it was a few days before her father sobered up enough to realize his role in her death. Overcome with guilt and the ravages of his years of drinking, he followed his daughter to her grave a few months later.

The old house stood empty for some time afterward, as there were no next of kin. A few tenants took the house, but none stayed very long. They complained of mysterious crying sounds and a grotesque female apparition peeking into the windows. Within a month, the teacher at the school left suddenly, claiming that strange shadows repeatedly darkened the classroom windows. About the same time, claims were made that a glowing translucent orb could be seen hovering behind one of the tombstones on dark, rainy nights.

Things had just begun to settle down when Jack Belcho, a young African American farm laborer, reported a most peculiar event. Jack lived outside the village, near the tollbooth for the Red Bank–Middletown turnpike. He had worked late that night caring for a sick horse on a farm that was located to the west. He wasn't certain of the time as he approached the village but assumed it must have been late, as there was not a single light on in any of the houses along Kings Highway. Then, he heard the clock on the tavern strike midnight. As he approached the darkened school building, he heard a peculiar noise, something he couldn't identify. It was something between a gasp and squawk. He hesitated for a moment and then trudged onward, anxious to get home. Although it wasn't cold, he shivered a bit and pulled his coat more tightly against his body.

He glanced at the cemetery to his left and then back at the road ahead. There, just before him on the road, was a dark object that spread the width of the highway. He had stepped onto the dark spot before he realized that it was a shadow. He realized at once that it was not a normal shadow; it was exceptionally dark and threatening. Jack himself later described it as being "dark as coal tar." At that instant, his throat contracted, and his neck was clutched by what felt like cold, clammy fingers. An icy breath seemed to suck the air from his lungs. He raised his hands to his throat, but there was nothing there. Yet, he could still feel an icy compression around his windpipe. He jerked his head to the side and glanced at the cemetery. He gurgled in horror at what he saw. Above every headstone appeared a solitary human hand, waving frantically at him, beckoning him to come that way.

It was getting harder to breathe; Jack forced in a gulp of air and looked back to the cemetery. A murky swirl of light moved to and fro among the graves, throwing a peculiar greenish glow over the entire burial ground. From each headstone arose a whirling, hazy cloud that morphed into a corpse right before his eyes. One after another, the grotesque figures rose into the air, where they hovered for a moment. After uttering a mournful wail, they vanished. From somewhere and everywhere, Jack could hear the echo of a throng of people weeping, as if there had been a great tragedy. Using his last ounce of energy, Jack thrust his body from the grip of the shadow and staggered away from the darkness. In that instant, the grip about his throat loosened and was gone. He took a deep breath and glanced toward the cemetery. The apparition had disappeared. The hands, the bodies, the lights and the sounds had vanished. The cemetery looked blissfully peaceful. The tombstones, lined in neat rows, were barely visible in the moonlight. Jack turned and looked back at the peculiar shadow, and for the first time, he realized that the darkness took the form of a coffin lid. He took off as fast as his legs could carry him, and he never looked back.

Afterward, Jack tried to recount his experience around the village to anyone who would listen, but few believed him. They all assumed that he had simply had too much to drink. But Jack knew what he had experienced, and he never again walked by the cemetery at night.

Just as we cannot deny parts of written history simply because we do not like or understand them, how can we deny these accounts of the supernatural that were archived by our ancestors? After all, these most peculiar events are a part of the heritage and deliciously rich history of Middletown Village.

15

THE WOMAN IN BLACK

For those who can remember, the 1960s were, as Charles Dickens wrote in the opening to *A Tale of Two Cities*, "the best of times... [and] the worst of times, it was the age of wisdom, it was the age of foolishness, it was the epoch of belief, it was the epoch of incredulity, it was the season of Light, it was the season of Darkness." At the beginning of the decade, the youngest man ever elected to the presidency moved into the White House with his young wife and small children. During the 1960s, man walked on the moon for the first time, Martin Luther King Jr. led nonviolent protests for civil rights and the birth control pill became readily available for the first time. As color televisions began filling American homes, the first ever Super Bowl was televised across the nation. Johnny Carson popularized *The Tonight Show*, the Beatles appeared on *The Ed Sullivan Show* and the nightly news carried the horrific scenes of the war in Vietnam, further dividing the American public. Before the decade ended, both the young president and Martin Luther King Jr. would be assassinated. There were violent antiwar protests, anti–civil rights atrocities, a cold war with Russia and an international fear of nuclear obliteration.

On the homefront, the 1960s brought major change to American fashion. The mini skirt appeared in 1965, followed by tie-dye shirts, jeans as a principal attire and an overall diverse approach to fashion that the young embraced and the old folks abhorred. These were the days of Andy Warhol's *Campbell's Soup Cans*, VW bugs painted in rainbows and psychedelic everything. It was also the era in which marijuana was called grass, fathers shouted at their sons about their long hair and people attended a legendary music festival called Woodstock. Red Bank prospered during the 1960s; storefronts were filled with the latest fashions, home goods and technologies. People still shopped on Friday nights and Saturday mornings. Broad Street hummed with the sounds of jingling cash registers, shoppers and high-powered car engines.

No one could recall exactly when the woman in black first appeared, but by the time her reoccurring presence was noted, it was agreed that she had been there for several months. A beautiful young woman arrived early every Saturday morning on Broad Street and spent the day walking slowly up and down both sides of the street. She was an attractive young woman dressed in the latest British "mod" fashion.

She first appeared as if she were a fashion model straight out of Great Britain. Her makeup was immaculate, and her black leather outfit was upscale and chic. It was perfectly coordinated with her tall leather boots, dark beret and oversized sunglasses. At first, people thought she was a model hired by local clothing stores to advertise their latest inventory. Others insisted she was a college student who was home for the weekend. Still others were certain she was a British au pair or a nanny from a nearby estate. She neither spoke nor made eye contact with anyone. Her face remained expressionless, never smiling or frowning.

Each Saturday, her routine was the same. She just appeared and sauntered up and down Broad Street. She never entered any stores or businesses, and she was never seen stopping for food or visiting a restroom. For a long time, people simply ignored her.

After a while, people noticed a change in her appearance. Ever so slowly, her trendy outfit gave way to dark ill-fitting and rather shabby clothing. Her feet, no longer in fashionable boots, dragged along the pavement in bulky clogs, which made a scraping sound as she passed. The black leather was gone, replaced with an unkempt black cape over a long black dress. Her once immaculate fingernails were smeared with a black nail polish. Her hair grew longer and longer until it trailed off her back like a mane. What could be seen of her face took on a grayish cast, which developed into a definite violet hue. Around the same time, her lips slowly shriveled into thin serpentine lines. In fact, her entire body seemed to shrink until she was just a shell within the baggy folds of her dark garb. Her gait noticeably slowed, but her pace remained steady and determined.

The identity of Red Bank's woman in black remains a mystery, even today. *From www. oldbookillustrations.com.*

Despite Red Bank's small size, no one knew her name or where she lived. No matter who you asked, no one could recall having ever seen her before anywhere in town. To make matters even more bizarre, no one ever saw her arrive on Broad Street. She didn't seem to drive a car, nor did anyone seem to drop her off. She would just suddenly appear early each Saturday, regardless of the weather. Neither rain, snow, wind nor a nor'easter deterred her.

It wasn't long before adults and children alike openly stared at her. Young children gawked and sometimes broke into tears, believing she was a witch. They clutched their mothers when they passed her on the street, and they often pointed a tiny finger in her direction. If she ever noticed, she never responded. Older and braver youngsters attempted to talk to her, without success. She ignored anyone who greeted her or attempted to stop her in the street. Even when teenagers taunted her, she remained silent. When approached by well-meaning adults who offered her shelter during a storm, she hurried away without speaking.

People sometimes stopped on street corners in small groups to discuss the unusual woman. There were two schools of thought: one believed her to be mortal and another deemed her to be an apparition of some sort. Yet, the grapevine abounded with explanations of the woman in black.

One group said she was a teen who had turned to drugs, and as her addiction worsened, so did her appearance and behavior. Their supposition was that she wandered in a drug-induced haze. Others claimed that she was most certainly the child of a well-known local mental patient who had committed suicide a few years earlier, abandoning the five-year-old child. They believed her wanderings were attempts to find her deceased mother. Still another claim was that she had lived in Red Bank as a youngster, but she was a peculiar girl who was sent away by her parents. They declared she was deeply disturbed and was merely trying to find her childhood home. Others had a more contemporary explanation; this group insisted that she was engaged to a young man who was drafted and sent to Vietnam. When he failed to return home, she took on this silent vigil as a protest of the draft system and the ongoing war.

There was a sizeable group who had a more paranormal approach to the case. Since witchcraft flourished in the 1960s, there was a contingent that believed she was indeed a witch. Although, that didn't explain why she kept up her lengthy vigil in Red Bank. There were several groups that felt she was most certainly the specter of a young wife who had spent many years searching for her lost husband. In one version of her story, he was run over by a horse and carriage on Broad Street many years before, and he was so disfigured that she could not recognize him. She didn't believe the dead man could be her husband, so she searched on for him. Another story said her husband died in a fire on Broad Street and she searched for his remains. Another said he was a soldier lost in World War II. Yet others claimed that he was a drunk and a womanizer who had simply left her and that she was spending eternity trying to bring him back home.

Still others believed her to be a supernatural spirit and insisted that she was a warning specter from Mother Earth. They believed that nuclear war was imminent and that the Mother Earth specter was in mourning for the coming end of civilization. A similar theory was that the very act of the young woman morphing into the old crone was a premonition of mankind's coming extinction. Despite all these theories, no evidence has ever been discovered to support any of the many explanations of the woman in black.

One Saturday, just before the new decade began, she simply failed to arrive. She was never seen again. We may never know the name of the silent figure in black who patrolled Broad Street in the 1960s or even if she was a spectral or physical being. Perhaps it is just as well. Allowing Red Bank's woman in black to remain anonymous and thus shelter her personal secret may leave us seeking closure, but perhaps it is a kindness we need to offer this unknown lady—or nameless specter.

16

THE GHOSTLY REVENGE
OF INDIAN JACK

By the early 1800s, the shores of the Navesink were home to an assortment of farms, plantations and estates. The farm crews were composed of enslaved people, indentured servants and freed people who were often day workers on local farms. A myriad of folk legends and tales circulated among both the workers and the landed gentry. Stories of ghosts and supernatural phenomena were published in the *Daily Register* by such prominent people as Judge George C. Beekman. In February 1895, he related a peculiar event that occurred years earlier near his estate. The story is made more tragic by the fact that it occurred on December 24, 1823, a day before Christmas.

The Christmas season is perceived by most to be a colorful, fun-filled period of glittering trees, gifts and endless celebrations. During the early years of the Navesink region's history, Christmas was no less important but was observed quite differently. The religious significance of Christmas was paramount across all classes of people. The middle and upper classes celebrated the holiday season with sumptuous feasts, gift-giving and lively parties and games. For the poorer classes, it was perhaps the one day of the year when food was plentiful. Families saved their pennies so they could have a bountiful holiday meal. It may have been the one day of the year when even a farmhand or an enslaved person might have a day of rest.

On the dawn of December 24, 1823, the workers on a farm just north of the river in Middletown began their task of threshing wheat. At the time, the job of threshing, or separating the grains of wheat from its husky covering, had to be done by hand. It was backbreaking work. After the grain was spread on the barn floor, the farmworkers beat the grain using handheld flails. These long poles were attached to a heavy club by a short chain and were difficult to use. One of the workers, a freed man John Henry, was particularly skilled in this craft. It was said he could produce nearly twice the amount of grain as other farmhands. As a result, he was always in demand for local farmers at threshing time. John was a quiet, hardworking family man who, in only one year of freedom, managed to build a small home for his young family in Red Bank.

John was part of the threshing crew that December day. As usual, he completed more than his share of the work before quitting time. It was the custom for the farmer to provide workers with a hot dinner and, sometimes, a warm bed at the end of a day's work. On that day, John quickly finished his meal ahead of the others. He told the farmer that he would go back out to the barn and finish the remaining work so that he could spend Christmas Day with his family. The farmer happily agreed. As the other workers headed home, they heard the steady echo of threshing coming from the barn. All through the evening, the farmer could hear the unceasing *thwack-thwack* of John Henry's flail. It was well after 11:00 p.m. before the barn was silent.

The next morning, as the farmer and his family prepared for their Christmas meal, John's wife appeared at the farm looking for her husband. He had not returned home the previous night. As it was unlike him to stay out all night, she was exceedingly distressed. A search of the barn found no trace of him. John Henry had simply vanished. During the next week, John Henry's friends searched for him but to no avail. The only peculiarity in the area was a complaint that a rowboat had been stolen from Compton's Creek. Yet, no one could believe that he had run off and left his wife and children. He owned his little house and adored his youngsters.

The following week, a bloated, disfigured body was discovered floating in the creek. At first, everyone thought the mystery had been solved and that John Henry had indeed taken off in the rowboat and somehow drowned. The crabs and eels had so mutilated the face that identification was not possible. But a closer inspection of the body revealed that its clothes could not belong to John Henry. The corpse was a much larger local man named Indian Jack.

Within a week, there had been two mysterious deaths. It was further known that the two men had once been enslaved under the same master at a nearby farm. Indian Jack had been on the estate several years before John Henry arrived. John was a reserved man who quietly did his work and caused no problems, and he often helped others with their tasks. Indian Jack, however, was quite the opposite. He was outspoken, rebellious and anxious to avoid his work, often pushing it off onto others.

Both men were promised their freedom after seven years if they completed their tasks without issue. John Henry easily completed this requirement and was freed in 1822. Jack, however, was still enslaved after twenty-eight years of service due to his bad temper and belligerent manner. It was common knowledge that Indian Jack was outraged when John Henry gained his freedom while he remained enslaved. Although John Henry had remained in the area, it was not believed that they had had any contact after he left the estate.

For nearly a full year, the mystery went unsolved, as no one believed the two deaths were related. In the days preceding Christmas 1824, the same farm was in the middle of threshing season. Just before Christmas Day, a local farmhand known as Harry hiked over to the farm, eager to join in the threshing the following day. It grew late, and he didn't arrive at the farm until around 11:00 p.m. Not wanting to wake the farmer and his family, he decided that he would just sleep in the barn and be ready for the next day's work. He climbed into the soft hay in the loft and covered himself with a horse blanket. Soon, he fell asleep.

Sometime after midnight, Harry was awoken by a loud thumping and a tremor that shook the planks of the hayloft. Tossing aside his blanket, he crept over the edge of the loft and looked down onto the barn floor. A soft yellow glow from a lantern cast a dim light on the grain that was strewn across the floor. Harry couldn't believe his eyes, for there stood John Henry, threshing the grain for all he was worth. Over and over, his muscular arms raised the flail in the air and then quickly brought it down with loud *thwack*. There was no doubt that it was John Henry, the missing farmhand.

As Harry stared at the incredible sight, the small barn door opened, and a taller, much larger man entered. He wore tattered work clothes, and in his hand, he carried a large axe. Although his face was smeared in rage, Harry recognized him at once. But it couldn't be; everyone knew that Indian Jack was dead. In one swift motion, Indian Jack crept up behind John Henry and buried the axe in his head. John crumpled to the floor. A scream began in Harry's throat, but only a gurgle escaped. The culprit took no notice of Harry, smiling at his achievement. He picked up a spade, moved to the far side of the barn floor and began ripping up the planks. When he had opened a space of floor about five feet by three feet wide, he grabbed a shovel and began digging a hole in the soft soil. When the cavity was about four feet deep, he scooped up the body and dumped it in. He tossed the axe and John Henry's flail in on top. After spitting on the remains, he refilled the hole and shoved the floorboards together. Tossing the tools aside, he quickly left the barn.

Harry was frozen in terror and afraid to leave the safety of the hayloft. He lay shivering in the dark for hours. At the first streaks of dawn, he ran to the house and told the farmer what he had seen. At first, the farmer accused him of being drunk, but he knew Harry to be a decent worker who was not prone to storytelling or exaggeration. When the farmer inspected the barn, everything was in its place until Harry called him over to the side where he had witnessed the burial. The farmer peered at the wooden floor; it had indeed been ripped up and re-laid. Using the same spade and shovel that Indian Jack had used the previous night, they opened the floor and began digging in the soft soil. There, they discovered a large rusty axe and John Henry's wooden flail resting on top of a decomposed body. The wound on the back of its head was a perfect match for the axe left in the grave.

As word spread of the grisly discovery, numerous sightings of Indian Jack were reported. Although none were substantiated, the farm soon acquired a reputation for being haunted. Local farmhands refused to work in the barn. In a few short years, the farmer lost the property and moved away. The aging barn stood empty and deserted for many years. Locals maintained that each

The old barn may still hold the spirits of Indian Jack and his victim, John Henry. *From www. freerangestock.com.*

year, as Christmas approached, the sounds of threshing resonated from the barn. Although no one reported any visual contact with the specter, many swear to have heard the *thwack-thwack* of a flail on the barn floor. Believers contended that it was indeed John Henry completing his chores so that he could be home in time for Christmas.

Perhaps you don't believe this tale. Maybe you are a person who needs to see it to believe it. You may want to locate the ruins of the barn and spend your Christmas Eve waiting in the cold and dark for the threshing to begin. It would indeed be a most unusual Christmas adventure. You may even be witness to the ghost of John Henry as he works. If you do, don't forget to wish him a Merry Christmas.

17

STRANGE HAPPENINGS IN OLE BALM HOLLOW

U ntil the nineteenth century, Balm Hollow, the portion of Middletown just northwest of the Navesink, was known as Blem Hollow. If we follow Oak Hill Road from where it intersects with Route 35 for two more miles westward, the road becomes Balm Hollow Road. The route traces along the valley floor until it reaches Red Hill Road, where it rises near Deep Cut Park. Today, locals think of it as one of the most desirable addresses in Monmouth County. But this was not always the case. Few are aware of the mysterious happenings that have occurred in the hollow since its history has been recorded. As early as the 1880s, the *Daily Register* published accounts of strange events in the region. In 1887, Judge George C. Beekman, who was also a local historian, wrote that Balm Hollow was one of the most haunted places in America. He noted that the hauntings had occurred even before the arrival of the European settlers.

The earliest passages through the hollow were mere footpaths used by local Native American tribes. In colonial times, a single track remained, with thick virgin forest on both sides. At many points, the tops of the trees grew together, forming a canopy over the path and shielding the path from daylight. At night, it became a dark and foreboding place. Before the arrival of the European settlers, Monmouth County was inhabited by a Native American tribe called the Lenni Lenape. Although the Lenape settled in the region, they did not establish settlements within the hollow itself. They avoided hunting there or traveling to the valley if at all possible. They insisted

Balm Hollow has been the site of spirits that cannot be identified or explained. *From George Cruickshank, www.oldbookillustrations.com.*

that the hollow was an evil place with a malevolent history that threated anyone traveling there.

The Lenape told of an old native man named Cokonkqua, a well-known hermit and wizard. He was the only person who resided in the valley. It was said that he recited incantations to an evil spirit who, in turn, gave Cokonkqua the gift of foretelling the future. But this gift did not come without a price. On certain nights, it was said Cokonkqua would sacrifice infants or small children and smear the blood on a mysterious tree deep in the forest. Cokonkqua gained fame for his predictions when he successfully predicted that a great canoe would come out of the water with men who had no color. He warned that these men would destroy the Lenape people. A few days after the prediction, the tribe reported the arrival of the first settlers. Cokonkqua then mysteriously disappeared, leaving his evil spirit to inhabit the hollow.

According to both native and early Dutch reports, the sound of crying children reverberated through the woods on particularly moonless nights. The Lenape believed that, should you hear the cries, then one of your own household would soon follow the crying child to the grave. While some settlers thought the native tales were silly superstitions, others confirmed that they heard the inexplicable sounds emanating from the deep forest. Although the settlers began using the route more frequently, they avoided the valley at night. One report came from a farmer who was delayed doing business in the village and was forced to travel the route after dark.

It was a warm summer night; the sounds of chirping and buzzing insects and the rustle of leaves echoed along the path. When the farmer's wagon reached the bottom of the hollow, his docile horses stopped short. He tried repeatedly to force them ahead, but they refused. The farmer searched for what was frightening the horses but found nothing. He could find no reason for their fear. Even if he applied the whip, the horses would not budge. They merely whinnied and snorted in fear. Even when he tried to walk the horses by holding their bridles, they jerked away, wild-eyed and trembling. It was then he realized that all the sounds of the forest had been stilled. There was only total silence; the wind had stopped, and the usual sounds of insects and woodland animals were gone. He finally turned the horses and retreated up the hill until he was well out of the hollow. He rested the horses and slept in his wagon that night. After dawn, he renewed his journey and passed through the valley without any further incident.

Another account came from a respected local physician who was called out one night to an emergency at a local farm. Although he did not normally use the path through the hollow at night, it was by far the shortest route to his destination, and time was of the essence. As he hurried along the path, he saw a lone man on horseback moving slowly ahead. He was surprised to see another traveler and was pleased for the company through the dark hollow. He nudged his horse forward to catch up to the rider. He called out, but the rider did not respond. He tried again, "Hello! I say, it's a cold night for travel, don't you think?" But still, there was no answer. The rider never turned to look back or pay any attention to his call. Seeing that the path ahead was narrow, and he could not pass the slow-moving rider, he called out again, "Sir, could I pass, please? I am a doctor on an emergency call." There was no response. The rider made no effort to move aside to allow the doctor to pass.

Finally, in frustration, the doctor stretched out his arm to the rider. "Sir, I do need to pass," he said, as he tapped the rider on the shoulder with his riding crop. The crop made a swishing sound as it passed through the rider completely. Instantly, both the horse and rider vanished. The startled doctor quickly nudged his horse into a gallop. The rhythmic clopping of his horse's hooves on the frozen earth was reassuring, as he tried to concentrate on the sound instead of the strange phantom rider he had encountered. It was only when he pulled up in front of the farmhouse and his horse stopped that he remembered the horse in the valley had made no such clopping sound as it traveled along the pathway. In fact, there had been no noise at all.

A few years later, another tragedy occurred in the valley. In 1815, a freed man named Samuel Herd purchased a parcel of land in the hollow. He was pleased with his purchase, as it was much cheaper than much of the land around his homestead. He was a hardworking, quiet man who built a cabin for his family near an estate where he worked as a foreman. One morning, he was discovered two hundred feet from his front door, beaten and bleeding with a length of rope around his neck. There were no witnesses, and the murder went unsolved. It would be two years before any clues would arise as to the mysterious death of Samuel Herd.

In the fall of 1817, two sailors came ashore after a lengthy sea voyage with plans to travel across the hollow to visit family on a farm near Holmdel. Daisy Dan, known for his flashy and colorful clothing, and his stern and heavy-drinking friend, Sam, were known as tough seamen. They were always looking for a challenge and equipped for any brawl that came their way. Any tittle tattle of evil spirits or supernatural events only made them laugh. As the pair traveled down the path that leads into Balm Hollow, a sudden thunderstorm arose. The men were searching for shelter when they came to the abandoned cabin of Samuel Herd. They quickly started a fire and opened a jug of applejack. Soon, the cabin was warm and snug. Sam drank his fill and fell into a heavy sleep by the fire, while Dan leaned his back against the hearth and slowly sipped his ale.

Suddenly, the front door crashed open. Dan felt himself frozen in place and could only gawk at the two figures in the doorway. He later recounted that one man was short and the other was much taller and wore heavy boots. Both had gray-greenish expressionless faces. The taller man filled the entire doorway, and the shorter one paused briefly at the door before shuffling across the room. A foul stench spread throughout the cabin as he walked noiselessly up the stairs. After a few minutes, the apparition eased back down the steps, and the two left the cabin. Finally able to move, Dan crept to the door and peeked out into the yard. About two hundred feet from the cabin, the men crouched behind a woodpile. Then, a black man walked slowly down the path toward the cabin. The men leapt from behind the woodpile and began beating him. Within minutes, they pulled a rope around his neck; the black man fell to earth, and the two men fled into the woods.

Dan wiped his eyes on his shirt sleeve; he could not believe what he had just seen. He ran to the spot where the man had fallen, but there was nothing there. He sprinted back to the cabin and tried to wake Sam. Dan was breathing so heavily that he could hardly speak, and it wasn't easy rousing Sam from his drunken sleep. Sam didn't believe Dan at first. He attributed Dan's story to too much drinking. It took Dan the remainder of the night to convince Sam of what he had seen. When they finally arrived in Holmdel and shared the story, the locals laughed at them, considering it to be a tale of a couple of drunken sailors.

This was not the last extraordinary event reported from the hollow. Early twentieth-century reports describe that malevolent foxlike beasts were spotted reclining on fallen logs within the valley forest. Others recounted that red-eyed creatures with fierce expressions followed unsuspecting travelers. Other tales include the wails of a child in distress wafting through the woods. When anyone followed the sounds, they were led deeper and deeper into the woods until they were entangled in a quagmire of undergrowth, causing the victim to wander helplessly until dawn. Today, the quiet of the hollow is permeated by the revving of automobile engines and the inevitable ringing of mobile devices. So, we must consider if the history of Balm Hollow is mere folklore or if the noise of modern America masks the echoes of the past. It is hard to say.

18

THE GUYON POINT PHANTOM

Guyon Point, located on the northern shoreline of the Navesink, lies just off Navesink River Road in Middletown. Nearly opposite of Fair Haven's Lewis Point, Guyon Point juts into the river, providing panoramic views of the river and southern shoreline. The point is named for James Guyon Timolat, whose opulent summer estate, the Riverside, once encompassed the entire point. Although it is no longer one single estate, the point remains an elite neighborhood of impressive residences.

For decades, numerous accounts of peculiar events at the site have circulated along the riverfront. One legend shared by multiple witnesses describes the occasional sighting of an old weathered rowboat found just off Guyon Point. Witnesses claim to have seen an aged rowboat floating aimlessly in the early morning, just as the fog is lifting from the river. A hunched-over old man is said to be grasping the side of the old boat as he peers intently into the water. Witnesses claim he seems to be calling out, although not a sound can be heard. If approached by another craft, the apparition disappears. Several witnesses insist that the specter is a grandfather from the mid-1900s who lost his grandson in a fishing accident many years ago.

Ernest had lived and worked on the river his entire life, so when he reached middle age, he was delighted when he secured a job as the caretaker of the massive estate on Guyon Point. The grounds were huge, and there was always something to do, but he didn't mind. The owners frequently travelled and were usually gone the entire winter. Ernest maintained the grounds, did odd carpentry and kept fires in the big house to ward off the damp during their absence. Ernest often said that the best part of the job was the little cottage on the estate that came with the job. With his children grown, it was perfect for him and his wife. They loved the waterfront clapboard bungalow, which was located some distance from the manor house on a small cove.

Even after many years, Ernest never lost his love of the river nor his respect for its power. Every summer, his grandson came to visit for several weeks. They spent many happy hours fishing and crabbing along the shore of the Navesink. The young boy constantly begged his grandfather to take him out in the boat so that they could catch "a really big fish." Ernest told his grandson, Paul, that they could only go off Guyon Point into the deeper water when he had learned to swim.

"But I just want to fish!" the boy pestered.

"When you can swim, young man; not until then," was the unchanging reply.

The year he was about to turn six, the boy arrived with exciting news. He told his grandparents that he had finally learned to swim. He described in detail the swimming lessons and demonstrated with his arms the different swim strokes he had mastered. True to his word, the very next day, his grandfather dragged the old rowboat down to the riverbank. The two loaded up their fishing tackle and a jar of clam worms and set out across the channel. They rowed to a spot just off Guyon Point, where the water was known to be particularly deep. The boy was determined that they would catch a snapper or a striped bass for their supper. They cast their lines into the deep water and waited. In a moment or two, something tugged on the boy's line, bending his pole toward the surface of the water. The boy grabbed the pole with both hands as his grandfather shouted to him to set the hook by jerking the pole upward. The boy grunted as he yanked his pole skyward.

"Now, start reeling it in!" his grandfather called. It took all the boy's strength to hold onto the pole with one hand and turn the crank on the reel at the same time. After what seemed like a lengthy struggle, a giant silver body flashed above the water.

The boy screeched, "Look! I caught—"

For just a moment, his grip loosened on the pole. He saw his mistake in an instant, but it was too late. The great fish dove to the bottom, yanking the boy over the side of the boat and into the water with a great splash. Ernest reached out to grab the boy but caught only some briny spray.

Expecting the boy to pop to the surface, the grandfather chuckled as he peered at the water. But then, there was nothing. There was no flailing or splashing—not even a bubble. Ernest shouted out the boy's name. He yanked off his shoes and dove into the water. He dove as deeply as he could but saw no sign of his grandson. He kept returning to the surface for air and dove again and again into the depths. The water was deep there, and he could not reach the bottom. The commotion alerted other fishermen, who came to his aid, but there was no sign of the boy. The body was never found.

Now, it is reported that on certain mornings, just as the fog is lifting, the apparition of the rowboat can be seen off Guyon Point. A frantic grandfather still searches in vain for his lost grandson. As soon as the sun is bright, the apparition disappears. Records from the investigation of the incident reveal that the boy had fibbed to his grandfather. He had not learned to swim; he had just wanted to go fishing.

19
THE SERPENT OF THE NAVESINK

The summer of 1889 was long remembered by locals along the Navesink River for more than its soaring temperatures and unrelenting humidity. All along the riverbank, discerning Victorian homes spread their windows wide, attempting to catch a bit of a cooling sea breeze. Before the end of summer, locals had much more to gossip about than the weather.

On a scorching summer Sunday, four Red Bank businessmen boarded the yacht *Tille S.* and headed out of Red Bank to enjoy a cooling afternoon on the bay near Highlands Beach. It was nearly dark when they began the trip homeward. With a full moon providing ample visibility for the journey, the skipper, Marcus P. Sherman, minded the tiller. His friends Lloyd Eglinton, Stephen Allen and William Tinton settled in the bow to keep watch for floating debris ahead. They were in fine spirits, enjoying the stiff summer breezes as they rounded the Highlands and headed for Red Bank.

Suddenly, Eglinton leapt to his feet, shouting and waving his arms in warning to Sherman. "Hard to port!" he shrieked. Sherman pulled hard on the rudder, and the boat veered toward shore as he cut the engine. At that moment, a huge dark mass, serpentine in shape, swam in a snake-like rhythm toward the boat. The men's attempts to speak were merely gasps and stifled moans. As the creature passed the bow, it raised its head slightly and gave a mighty growl. In an instant, it disappeared into the depths. Speechless, they watched as the wake from the creature eased slowly toward Hartshorne Cove. Then, it disappeared into the dark water.

Once the men regained their composure, they began sharing their descriptions with one another. They established that the head resembled a bulldog, with large eyes the size of silver dollars. On the very top of its head were rounded horns, like growths jutting out just above its eyes. Bristles traced the upper lip of the creature, and the nostrils were large and flattened. The men agreed that the tapered body was about fifty feet long and that it had a pointed tail.

Although the four were reluctant to report the sighting at first, they discovered that many others had reported encounters with the creature. The *Daily Register* reported that over a dozen boaters had recounted seeing the beast in the spring and summer of 1889. These sightings occurred in both the northern branch of the river, known as the Navesink, and the southern tributary, known as the Shrewsbury. Many locals called it the Shrewsbury Serpent; others insisted it was the Serpent of the Navesink.

While this may be one of the most noted descriptions of the creature, earlier accounts from 1879 claim that a three-hundred-foot sea monster was sighted off Sandy Hook. This account is given credence, as it was described in detail, complete with hand-drawn illustrations, in the December 1879 issue of *Scientific American*. Like the creature observed by the Red Bank crew, this monster had a snake-like body and a square cranium with horn-like projections on the top of its head. The Sandy Hook creature was described to be much larger, and for a time, it was believed to be a giant squid. Over the next few years, sightings of unusual sea creatures abounded in this area of the Atlantic coast.

Throughout the following decades, fishermen and boaters periodically claimed to have encountered some sort of marine beast in the Navesink. In August 1963, the *New York Times* reported that a serpent-like creature was sighted near the mouth of the Navesink in Sandy Hook Bay. The eyewitnesses included Dr. Lionel Wolford, the director of the U.S. Fish and Wildlife Research Center, who identified the creature as a forty-foot invertebrate that moved through the water in an undulating fashion. To this day, local fishermen exchange tales and sightings; boaters scan the water on dark nights hoping for even a glimpse of the Shrewsbury Serpent. While no specimen has yet to be discovered, who is to say what lies beneath the tidal waters of the beautiful twin rivers?

20
TALES AND YARNS FROM WHIPPOORWILL VALLEY

hile many accounts of mysterious events in the Navesink region
may be unfamiliar to many, longtime residents are aware of the
peculiar reputation of Whippoorwill Valley Road in Middletown.
About a mile north of the river, this scenic country lane meanders through
woodlands, rolling hills, horse farms and great estates between Chapel Hill
Road and Kings Highway. Even today, portions of Whippoorwill Valley
Road remain heavily wooded. An untamed dirt road is the only path through
one section of the valley, and it is only passable with a sturdy vehicle. It is a
discomforting ride, even in the daytime, and it is certainly not for the faint
of heart. As in the recent past, today, the road is a popular hangout spot for
teenagers and is a popular territory for paranormal investigators. There are
many reports of supernatural activities reported by word of mouth, print
and, now, internet postings.

Assertions that the road is cursed due to a history of devil worship in
the woods have endured for many years. Some reports insist that the devil
himself claimed the area as his own, and he is said to roam the area,
protecting this tract for his followers. For many years, accounts circulated of
satanic rituals, blood sacrifices and the sounds of dissonant chants wafting
through the forest. Although no reliable account of the rituals exists today,
we do know that such groups did indeed utilize the isolated area. During the
late 1970s, ruins of an abandoned building gave evidence that some form
of satanic activity occurred there. Multiple reliable sources identified the
ruins of an abandoned building, in which the remains of a worn wooden

Sometimes, the trees on Whippoorwill Valley Road seem to be watching you. *From www. pixabayillustrations.com.*

Do not expect to travel alone as you pass through the lonely Whippoorwill Woodlands. *From www. commons.wikimedia.net.*

floor revealed a large pentagram within a perfect circle, as a hotspot for hauntings. On the adjacent wall, two upside-down Roman crosses flanked the pentagram. Within the same area, various satanic symbols and numbers could be seen scratched or painted on the weathered surfaces. The site is now a redeveloped private property, and it is assumed that those markings have been erased.

Another legend of the Whippoorwill Valley Road is based on a dark period in the area's local history. One account maintains that on moonless nights, an unsuspecting traveler may be waylaid by an opaque antique pickup truck. The truck suddenly appears in the narrowest section of the lane so that it is impossible to pass. Some reports claim that there is no driver at the wheel of the truck, while others insist that the truck is weighed down with dozens of Ku Klux Klansmen in full white garb. Of these reports, a few insist they were able to outrun the truck, and others claimed they were forced to turn around and escape the way they came.

As with much folklore, these accounts have a correlation with historical events in the region. It seems that the KKK was not so clandestine in this area. The history of the Klan in this region is well documented. It is quite possible that in its early days, when the Klan met secretly, it may have used this secluded area for its rendezvous. By the 1920s and into the early 1930s, the Klan was well entrenched and openly active in communities all along the Navesink. Large numbers of newspaper accounts, as well as published photographs, recount the meetings, cross burnings and parades through the streets of local communities. With our knowledge of the Klan's history in the area, we are left with a provoking question: What if the evil of the group was so strong that it managed to permeate the spatial energy of this twenty-first-century road? Are these apparitions just the tip of a more sinister evil in our midst? And do so many teenagers see the apparitions because the evil seeks out the young as a means to destroy all that is good?

Some of the best-known legends are centered on bridges and babies—and sometimes both. Today, the bridges along the road are so small that they are nearly undetectable. They are mere shallow platforms, covered in dirt and gravel over the small brooks. Yet, the folklore is rich with accounts of assorted sightings at these spots. One such tale is that of an infant thrown into the stream by a farmer who suspected his wife of having an affair. When she gave birth, the farmer claimed the infant looked like his wife's lover and drowned the child. One narrative claims that if you stand on the bridge late at night, you can hear the helpless child crying. Another asserts that if you stop your car on the bridge and get out, the baby will rise from its grave and push the car away from the grave site. Yet another related allegation is that if you stop your car on the bridge and hear the baby cry, the car will not start again. Only after you have sung a lullaby to the baby will your car start. There was never an infanticide recorded on Whippoorwill Valley Road or anywhere near the area. Yet, history is not always accurate. Such an event would likely have not been reported, or it may have been considered far too grisly to publicize.

In addition to the paranormal events discussed so far, the road is recognized for a series of singularly peculiar occurrences and apparitions. Many of these accounts have been passed down by word of mouth until recently, when one can find them cited in numerous paranormal websites and blogs. Both websites and popular regional magazines carry the reports of those who have claimed to have experienced paranormal events on

Whippoorwill Valley Road. Some discovered peculiar symbols carved on rocks and trees deep within the woods. Another described seeing a handmade wooden sign shaped like an arrow with the word "God" scrawled across its length pointing into a dense thicket. There are countless claims of finding unidentifiable relics, symbols and strange tools in the area. Still others insist they heard unearthly sounds and groans emanating from the road.

There are numerous reports of ghostly creatures in a variety of forms in the area. One is of a lone horseback rider who takes chase if an unsuspecting traveler tries to pass through the valley at night. Other sightings claim to have heard what sounded like a large creature running through knee-deep water in great haste. And one detailed testimony came from a local man who claimed to have seen Jesus dancing down the lonely road at dawn.

One recent account described the discovery of a rather grotesque-looking tree growing along the narrow lane. The tree, which has a twisted and gnarled trunk, as if nature was attempting to turn it into a pretzel, is malformed and rusty brown in color. The upper foliage is scant and drab, and the air around the tree is always damp and chilly. A closer inspection reveals what appears to be an image of a human being devoured by the trunk of the tree. When the same witness attempted to photograph the tree, his cell phone simply would not work. Not only was the camera function disabled, but there was no cell service anywhere near the tree. The phone did not function again until he had driven some distance away from the area.

So, before we make final judgements about Whippoorwill Valley Road and its long history of strange and peculiar events, perhaps it is best to take that dark ride and decide for ourselves.

BIBLIOGRAPHY

Newspapers and Periodicals

Asbury Park Journal
Asbury Park Press
Asbury Park Shore Press
Atlantic Highlands Journal
Atlantic Highlands Monmouth Press
Freehold Inquirer
Long Branch Daily Record
Long Branch Journal
Monmouth Democrat
Monmouth Star
New York Herald
New York Herald Tribune
New York Times
Red Bank Daily Register
Red Bank Daily Standard
Scientific American
Weird New Jersey

Books

Adelberg, Michael. *The American Revolution in Monmouth County*. Charleston, SC: The History Press, 2010.

Field, Van, and John Galluzzo. *New Jersey Coast Guard Stations and Rumrunners*. Charleston, SC: Arcadia Press, 2004.

Kimmel, Richard. *Folklore of the New Jersey Shore*. Atglen, PA: Stackpole Press, 2006.

Lindenroth, Matthew. *Prohibition on the North Jersey Shore*. Charleston, SC: The History Press, 2010.

Macken, Linda Lee. *Ghosts of the Garden State*. Forked River, NJ: Blackcat Books, 2001.

———. *Ghosts of the Jersey Shore*. Forked River, NJ: Blackcat Books, 2011.

———. *Haunted Monmouth County*. Forked River, NJ: Blackcat Books, 2014.

Mahon, T.J. *Golden Age of Monmouth*. Fair Haven, NJ: T.J. Mahon Publishing, 1964.

———. *Red Bank Graphic*. Fair Haven, NJ: T.J. Mahon Publishing, 1970.

Mappen, Marc. *Jerseyana: The Underside of New Jersey History*. New Brunswick, NJ: Rutgers Press, 1992.

Martinelli, Patricia, and Charles Stanfield. *Haunted New Jersey: Ghosts and Strange Phenomena of the Garden State*. Atglen, PA: Stackpole Press, 2014.

Methot, June. *Up and Down the River*. Navesink, NJ: Whip Publications, 1980.

Moss, George, Jr. *Nauvoo to the Hook*. Locust, NJ: Jervey Press, 1964.

———. *Steamboat on the Shore*. Sea Bright, NJ: Ploughshare Press, 1966.

Roberts, Russel, and Rich Youmans. *Down the Jersey Shore*. New Brunswick, NJ: Rutgers Press, 1994.

Securman, Mark, and Mark Morgan. *Weird New Jersey: Your Travel Guide to New Jersey's Local Legends and Best Kept Secrets*. New York: Barnes and Noble, 2003.

Stanfield, Charles. *Haunted Jersey Shore*. Atglen, PA: Stackpole Press, 2006.

Stockton, Frank. *Stories of New Jersey*. New Brunswick, NJ: Rutgers Press, 1991.

Underwood, Peter. *The Ghosts Hunter's Guide*. Poole, UK: Blandford Press, 1986.

Wilson, Harold. *The Jersey Shore: A Social and Economic History of the Counties of Atlantic, Cape May, Ocean, and Monmouth*. New York: Lewis Historical Publishing, 1953.

Libraries and Archives

Middletown New Jersey Public Library: Historical Archive
Monmouth County Historical Commission
Monmouth Country Library Eastern Branch Historical Archive
New Jersey State Library Historical Archive
Red Bank Public Library: The History Room (archive)

ABOUT THE AUTHOR

Patricia Martz Heyer, a longtime history buff and local resident, has written extensively for both children and adults throughout her career. Most recently, she has authored *Shark Attacks of the Jersey Shore: A History* (The History Press, August 2020), and another New York shark attack project is coming in 2021. She lives on the Narvarumsunk Peninsula with her husband and rescued black cat, Gracie.